THE BEST OF
Birds&Blooms®

contents

30

from the editor

Time flies when you're having

fun, and we've been having a lot of fun at *Birds & Blooms* magazine! Enjoy the latest in the world of birding and gardening from the past year with this brand-new edition of *The Best of Birds & Blooms*. The book is full of gorgeous photos, interesting features, DIY projects, bird-watching hot spots, expert birding advice, gardening know-how and much more. It also includes a bonus chapter on butterflies, bees and other insects as well as a native plants chart and plant zone maps.

Learn how to perk up spring landscapes with 14 flowering trees in "Branch Out With Blooms" (page 145). Discover secrets of bird courtship, including elaborate displays and romantic gestures, with "Love Is in the Air" (page 8). Check out birding hot spots from coast to coast to keep you busy bird-watching all year-round in "Follow that Bird!" (page 188).

That's just a sampling of what awaits you in this edition of *The Best of Birds & Blooms*. It's a collection every birder, gardener or nature lover is sure to appreciate now and for years to come.

Kirsten Sweet

Acting Editor, *Birds & Blooms*

Easy-to-Make Feeders (page 106)

COVERS: JOHN GILL (NORTHERN CARDINAL); STEVE AND DAVE MASLOWSKI (BLUE JAY); BILL LEAMAN/THE IMAGE FINDERS (ROSE-BREASTED GROSBEAK); MARIE READ (BALTIMORE ORIOLE); STEVE AND DAVE MASLOWSKI (YELLOW WARBLER); STEVE AND DAVE MASLOWSKI (AMERICAN GOLDFINCH); DANNY BROWN (RUBY-THROATED HUMMINGBIRD); GLENN BARTLEY (WESTERN

EDITORIAL

Editor-in-Chief Catherine Cassidy
Vice President, Content Operations Kerri Balliet
Creative Director Howard Greenberg

Managing Editor/Print & Digital Books Mark Hagen
Associate Creative Director Edwin Robles Jr.

Associate Editor Julie Kuczynski
Layout Designer Nancy Novak
Editorial Services Manager Dena Ahlers
Editorial Production Coordinator Jill Banks
Copy Chief Deb Warlaumont Mulvey
Copy Editor Chris McLaughlin
Contributing Copy Editors Kristin Sutter, Valerie Phillips
Business Architect, Publishing Technologies Amanda Harmatys
Solutions Architect, Publishing Technologies John Mosey
Business Analyst, Publishing Technologies Kate Unger
Junior Business Architect, Publishing Technologies Shannon Stroud
Editorial Services Administrator Marie Brannon
Editorial Business Manager Kristy Martin
Rights & Permissions Associate Samantha Lea Stoeger
Editorial Business Associate Andrea Meiers

Executive Editor Jeanne Ambrose
Acting Editor, *Birds & Blooms* Kirsten Sweet
Art Director, *Birds & Blooms* Sharon K. Nelson

BUSINESS
VP, Publisher Russell S. Ellis

TRUSTED MEDIA BRANDS, INC.
President & Chief Executive Officer Bonnie Kintzer
Chief Financial Officer Dean Durbin
Chief Marketing Officer C. Alec Casey
Chief Revenue Officer Richard Sutton
Chief Digital Officer Vince Errico
Senior Vice President, Global HR & Communications
Phyllis E. Gebhardt, SPHR; SHRM-SCP
General Counsel Mark Sirota
Vice President, Magazine Marketing Christopher Gaydos
Vice President, Operations Michael Garzone
Vice President, Consumer Marketing Planning Jim Woods
Vice President, Digital Product & Technology Nick Contardo
Vice President, Financial Planning & Analysis William Houston
Publishing Director, Books Debra Polansky

Pictured on the front cover:
Rose-breasted grosbeak, Bill Leaman/The Image Finders
Monarch on milkweed, Steve Bly/Getty

Pictured on the back cover:
Paper kite butterfly, Butterfly World
Yellow warbler, Steve and Dave Maslowski
Garden, Francis & Janice Bergquist

STEVE AND DAVE MASLOWSKI

the joys of
Bird-Watching

There's always more to learn about the world of birds. Read about courtship, eggs, molting, feet, albinism, extinct species and more! Plus, can you tell the difference between young and adult birds or East and West Coast species?

Love

When it comes to courtship, birds pull out all the stops, using elaborate displays to attract a potential mate and outdo the competition. Each species tackles this very important task differently. Here are some courtly behaviors to look for this spring.

By Ken Keffer

IS IN THE AIR

SANDHILL CRANE

Cranes are elegant dancers. Dancing peaks during mating season but can occur any time of year. Experts do not completely understand the behavior, but it seems to play a role in bonding. Mated sandhill cranes also sing a unison call during courtship. Curiously, young birds also dance—believed to be an important part of their motor development. Humans have admired crane dancing for centuries; many cultures have symbolic rituals that mimic the behavior.

Male house wrens use natural cavities and nest boxes to create partial nests for potential mates.

The male sharp-tailed grouse will try to tempt a mate by inflating the purple air sac on his neck.

HOUSE WREN

One of the most prolific backyard singers is the house wren, but a male's singing is mostly a territorial claim. To find mates, males must choose good nest sites. Wrens often nest close to people, so you're likely to hear them this spring. They use natural cavities, but they also like nest boxes. Males construct partial nests in multiple sites, and the females select from the offerings. When a female finds a suitable site, she mates with the owner.

SHARP-TAILED GROUSE

This grouse species uses a lek—a mating arena of sorts—where males perform to attract females. Male sharp-tailed grouse stick their pointed tails up, aim their wings down and inflate purple air sacs along their necks. Then they quickly shake and vibrate their entire bodies while cooing out. Females visit the lek during these displays and select a male to breed with. Prairie chickens have a similar dance. Sage grouse have air sacs on their chests, which they inflate and boom. No matter the species, a grouse display is always a sight to see.

RUFFED GROUSE

While grouse of the prairies gather on communal leks, the ruffed grouse of the northern woods has a solitary display. Perched on a downed log, the male, starting slowly at first but quickly accelerating, flaps his cupped wings, creating a deep whooshing that sounds like a tractor starting up on a cold morning. This short burst of chest drumming reverberates through the forest, which helps females find potential mates.

The ruffed grouse perches on a downed log and puffs up his feathers to almost double the normal size in a showy display to entice a mate and defend his territory.

When it's time to pair up, bald eagles begin courting potential companions in early spring, winter or even fall.

BALD EAGLE

The regal bald eagle puts on one of the most spectacular courtship shows. Mated partners lock talons in midflight and then spiral in a free-fall dive known as cartwheeling. Red-tailed and other hawks will cartwheel in courtship, too. Eagles often mate for life, and pairs will return to the same nests year after year. Male bald eagles help with nest construction and raising the eaglets.

SONG SPARROW

Some bird species have a single song that they perfect, but that isn't good enough for the aptly named song sparrow. Song sparrow males can sing as many as 20 different songs while defending territories and courting females. Some studies indicate that a female song sparrow chooses a mate based in part on his ability to learn new songs.

In a romantic gesture, male cardinals often fetch seeds and feed them to their mates during courtship and breeding.

Female Wilson's phalaropes have brighter, more vivid feathers than males.

NORTHERN CARDINAL

Male cardinals have bright red plumage that impresses females, but courting for this species goes deeper than surface attraction. Females sing along with the males during courtship. Experts believe the duet strengthens the bond. Listen for pure, repetitive whistling from cardinal pairs. Females sometimes call while on the nest. Males bring food to the females to ensure nesting success.

GREAT HORNED OWL

Like cardinals, great horned owls also perform a courtship duet. Owls are early nesters; listen for their characteristic hoots on cold, crisp winter nights. Female great horned owls are bigger than males, but males have larger voice boxes. When you hear them calling back and forth, try to pick up the male's deeper voice and the female's corresponding higher pitched hoots. Males assist throughout the entire nesting season and will bring food to the nest for the female and young.

WILSON'S PHALAROPE

Among many bird species, males and females have the same or similar feather markings. In several others, males have brighter plumage than females. Less common is when the female has the fancier feathers. This is true for the shorebird Wilson's phalarope, however. Spring females have vivid chestnut and black along the face and neck; males are more subtly colored. Females court multiple males during breeding season, and males incubate the eggs.

did you know?

Learn more about eggs—the beginning of every bird's life.

220 Brown-headed cowbirds deposit their eggs in other birds' nests. Cowbird eggs have been found in nests of more than 220 other species.

26 Large birds sit on eggs, too, so their eggs have to be strong enough to withstand the weight. It takes about 26 pounds of pressure to break a swan egg.

5 A single ostrich egg can weigh as much as 5 pounds.

40 A wood duck can lay up to 15 eggs in one nesting attempt, but a single nest may have as many as 40 eggs from more than one female.

Great gray owl protecting nest

1 Most songbirds lay one egg per day until their clutch is complete.

1/2 Rufous hummingbird eggs are ½ inch long and fit snugly in the 2-inch-wide nest, which usually holds two eggs.

4 Pale pink at first, tree swallow eggs turn white within four days.

2 American white pelicans lay two eggs per clutch. The young are able to squawk from inside their eggs if they're too hot or cold.

home *Tweet*

BUILT TO LAST

The grand champion nest builder is…the bald eagle! In 1963, an eagle's nest near St. Petersburg, Florida, was declared the largest at nearly 10 feet wide, 20 feet deep and over 4,400 pounds. That nest was extreme; most bald eagle nests are 5 to 6 feet in diameter and 2 to 4 feet tall. Nest construction can take three months. Eagles typically use the same nest every year, adding to it each season.

Eagles' nests are made of sticks with soft materials, like grass, moss and cornstalks, stuffed into the cracks.

home

From simple scrapes on the ground to elaborately woven structures, birds' nests are temporary yet meticulously built places to raise young. Learn about different housing styles and where various species choose to set up house.

By Ken Keffer

Once the eggs hatch, this hummingbird nest will stretch to accommodate the growing nestlings.

SMALL AND FLEXIBLE

It should come as no surprise that hummingbirds, our smallest birds, make the smallest nests. Hummingbirds build on top of tree branches, using plants, soft materials and spider webs. Ruby-throats decorate theirs with flakes of lichen. Anna's hummingbirds may lay eggs before a nest is completed, continuing to build the sidewalls during incubation. Most impressive is how these nests stretch. Hummingbirds usually lay a pair of eggs, the size of black beans, inside a nest about the diameter of a quarter. As the babies grow, the nest expands, keeping things tight and cozy.

It might take a female Altamira oriole three weeks to build a nest, which can be 2 feet long.

INTRICATE AND ELABORATE

Orioles are the seamstresses of the bird world. Their iconic pendant nests dangle from outermost tree branches. The nests are impossible to miss among barren winter branches and nearly as impossible to spot, surrounded by leaves, during the breeding season. Orioles use whatever material is available to stitch their bag nests—long grasses, twine, even horsehair. The nests are lined with soft materials such as plant fibers, feathers or animal wool. The Altamira oriole of extreme south Texas and Central America constructs one of the longest dangling nests, which can hang down more than 2 feet.

PRECARIOUS CLIFF SIDES

Huge colonies of murres and guillemots nest on rocky coastal cliffs. Most lack any structural nests, instead laying eggs that are extra pointy on one end. This shape helps the eggs pivot around the point instead of rolling over the edge. These ledge nesting sites are also more protected from predators. Cliff nesters can be found on coasts and inland. Lots of species, including condors, ravens and falcons, use cliffs, but they build stick nests in crevices.

Instead of building nests, thick-billed murres lay eggs on the narrow ledges of steep cliffs.

NO FUSS

It's the exception rather than the rule, but a few species of birds get away with building hardly any nest at all. This doesn't mean they are haphazard in their approach to laying eggs, though. Beach nesting birds—including black skimmers, many species of terns, and piping, Wilson's and other plovers—lay eggs in shallow depressions scraped out in the sand. The remarkable thing about the eggs of these species is their cryptic camouflage coloration. Eggs are often speckled and match the sandy granules of the makeshift nests. Sometimes these birds will line the shallow scrape with shells or sand to add to the camouflage. As beaches get more developed, some of these beach nesters have adapted to laying eggs on nearby rooftops.

Killdeers lay eggs directly on the ground.

Great horned owls reuse nests made by hawks, eagles or crows.

Least grebes build nests in shallow water, usually only 1 to 3 feet deep.

FLOATING NESTS

Some waterbirds, including many ducks, nest in upland grasslands far from water. Others, such as loons, grebes, coots and gallinules, nest directly on top of the water. Eggs will sink, so the birds build floating platform nests out of cattails, reeds, other aquatic vegetation or mud. They anchor the nests to emergent vegetation to conceal them and to keep them from drifting away.

POWER NESTING

It is hard to say officially *whoooo* lays the first eggs each year, but my pick for favorite nest is the great horned owl's. Sure, many species can begin nesting in January in southern states, but it is still winter in the northern states when great horned owls start incubating their eggs in nests made of sticks, often in trees. It's essential that these owls get an early start on nesting because the species is slow to hatch and fledge. It is remarkable to think of the owls sitting on eggs as snow piles up during frigid nights.

HIDDEN UNDERGROUND

Holes in trees and cacti are nest cavities; underground nests are burrows. Burrowing owls in Florida will sometimes dig their own burrow, while those in the West usually rely on spots excavated by prairie dogs, badgers, tortoises or other diggers. Other underground nesters include bank swallows, belted kingfishers and Atlantic puffins.

Burrowing owls nest in areas surrounded by bare soil or short grass.

BEST *feathered*

Male spotted sandpipers play a huge role in incubating eggs and caring for their young.

fathers

A tip of the hat to the hardest-working bird dads around!

By Kenn and Kimberly Kaufman

On Father's Day,

the bird dads in our backyard aren't kicking back and enjoying a warm summer day. A male song sparrow, flecked with brown and white, lands on a tree branch to sing between trips to a hidden nest where his hungry offspring wait for the next mouthful. Meanwhile, a flash of red on the opposite side of the hedge means a male northern cardinal is delivering dinner to his own eager brood.

Dads of some species of the bird world provide more than just meals, though. They help build nests, incubate eggs and stick around even after the moms have left. (To give credit where credit's due, there's no denying that female birds often wind up with more than their fair share of parenting duties. For example, male hummingbirds may be flashy, but they're not very helpful—they don't even stick around to watch the females raise their young.)

As a salute to the fathers with feathers that do help out around the nest, let's turn the spotlight on these hardworking parents.

Lending a Wing

A number of backyard bird dads, including cardinals and Baltimore orioles, spring into action once their babies are hatched, flying back and forth with food. Even after the youngsters have left the nest, bird dads feed them for several days to make sure they have the best chance of survival. And if the female starts working on a second nest before the previous brood is completely independent, the male may become a super dad and take on caring for the fledglings entirely on his own.

Many males are busy parents even before the eggs hatch. For example, a male American robin brings his

Sandhill cranes are dedicated dads. They keep their babies close and care for them for nearly a year.

No.1 BEST ALL-AROUND

№.1 BEST BUILDER

Male house wrens start building a few nests, and then the female chooses one and completes construction.

№.1 BEST INCUBATOR

Northern flicker fathers keep eggs warm throughout the night.

female partner bits of material as she constructs the nest. At dawn, he constantly sings from a high perch. It may be a little annoying for his human neighbors, but he's doing the important job of protecting his territory. Without his vigilant efforts, other robins might invade and eat all the juicy bugs and worms, making it harder for the robin parents-to-be to find enough food for their future nestlings.

Equal Partner Parenting

For some birds, like downy woodpeckers, parenting is a true partnership. Male and female downies work together to carve a nest hole in a dead tree trunk or limb, taking turns chiseling away to create a safe, secure cavity. They both incubate the eggs, too. Mom and Dad take turns during the day, but at night it's usually Dad who takes over. And once the babies have hatched, both parents help feed them. Sometimes the male downy woodpecker will end up feeding the young more than the female does.

Birds of prey, like hawks and owls, have a similarly balanced parenting style, although males and females take on different roles. Both red-shouldered hawk parents build the nest, for example, but only the female does the incubating and watches over the young

Snowy owls split the work. Males keep busy delivering food to the nest, and females watch the young.

No. 1 BEST PROVIDER

once the eggs hatch. The male isn't slacking off, though. It's his job to keep the food supply coming, first for the female as she sits on the eggs and then for the whole ravenous family.

Role Reversal

Some female birds aren't the type to sit on nests all day. Phalaropes—three species of small sandpipers—are a prime example of this parenting flip-flop. The females, who are more colorful than males, take the lead in courtship, and one female may have more than one mate. But whether she has one mate or several, she lays a clutch of four eggs for each of them, and leaves new dads to incubate eggs and raise young.

Spotted sandpipers, common in ponds and streams in most of North America, have a similar parenting technique, but for a long time scientists didn't realize it because the males and females look nearly identical. These days, we know that spotted sandpiper dads do most of the incubating and tending to the young. The moms are too busy laying clutches of eggs with other dads to help out!

Rad Dads

Whether they're endlessly hunting down food or shouldering all of the raising and rearing themselves, bird dads are pretty amazing. From strong nests to healthy fledglings, bird dads make it all possible.

DAD AWARDS

Birds that go beyond the call of daddy.

BEST BUILDER
The male house wren is serious about nest building, because it's what helps him attract a mate. He starts constructing a few nests at once, and his female partner chooses the most promising one and finishes it.

BEST INCUBATOR
Northern flicker fathers do the heavy lifting when it comes to keeping the eggs warm. Their incubating duties leave them sitting on eggs all night long and half the day as well.

BEST PROVIDER
While a snowy owl mom is busy with the nestlings, the dad brings food to keep everybody fed. If it's been a particularly good year, he may leave a large stockpile of dead lemmings and other rodents around the nest.

BEST ALL-AROUND PARENT
Not only do male sandhill cranes help with nest building, incubation and feeding their young, but families stick together through fall migration, winter and the beginning of spring migration. Young cranes learn and benefit from both parents.

Outgrowing

PEER THROUGH YOUR BINOCULARS
TO SEE IF YOU CAN SPOT THE
DIFFERENCES BETWEEN YOUNG
AND ADULT BIRDS.

BY KEN KEFFER

Summer is the season when juvenile birds develop their wing feathers in a process called fledging and begin to explore the world beyond the nest. It's a fantastic time to bird-watch, but a few of these youngsters are tricky to recognize, thanks to camouflage coloring. If you know what to look for, you can be ready when one flies across your path.

THE NEST

Notice the prominent spots on this juvenile robin's back.

AMERICAN ROBIN
Baby birds often don't resemble their parents, and young robins are a classic example. Like deer fawns, they have bold spots during their first summer, with buff speckling along their backs and breasts. Watch as they scamper across the lawn, mimicking the red-breasted adults as they hunt for worms and other invertebrates.

DOWNY WOODPECKER

You've probably seen black-and-white downy woodpeckers flying through your backyard, but during the summer months you may have noticed some with extensive red on their foreheads and crowns. These are young downies, and both sexes wear this red initially, although it's more widespread on males. (Adult female downy woodpeckers have no scarlet markings at all.) Use binoculars to observe the dark browns in the wings of these birds compared with the black feathers of the adults.

Identify growing downies by their red caps. Adult males (left) have smaller red patches.

BROWN-HEADED COWBIRD

Occasionally, something about a bird family doesn't seem quite right. Maybe a tiny yellow warbler is feeding a much larger bird, or a wood thrush has a tagalong with a thicker bill and streaky markings. Brown-headed cowbirds are nest parasites, which means females lay eggs in the nests of other species. They hatch quickly, and the host parents raise the larger, grayish-brown cowbird young. Many species involuntarily host cowbird eggs, so these young birds are always mismatched with the adults raising them.

A song sparrow feeds a much larger immature cowbird.

Young mountain bluebirds are gray-blue like their mothers.

BLUEBIRD

Bluebirds are related to robins, so it's no big surprise that most juveniles appear different from the adults. This difference is subtle on mountain bluebirds, where the bellies of young birds seem almost scalloped. But the closely related eastern and western bluebird juveniles have spotted backs to match their marked bellies. The blue tint of their wings and tails also helps ID them.

BLACK-CROWNED NIGHT-HERON

Once it's all grown up, this wetland species is quite stately, with thick black bills, ebony crowns and backs, and gray wings and bodies that fade into lighter-hued bellies. Young birds, however, appear more like bitterns than night-herons because of their broad brown streaks. Their bills have lots of yellow that slowly turns black. Eyes start off yellow-orange but gain richer color over time, eventually turning nearly red.

BROWN; JOHANN SCHUMACHER DESIGN; CAROL L. EDWARDS

Male American redstarts have bold black-and-orange coloring. But 1-year-old males (inset) are subtly colored, like females.

AMERICAN REDSTART

For this species of warbler, the resemblance between the young birds and the adult females continues beyond the first fall. During the second summer, a few black feathers show up on the males to set them apart from females, but it isn't until later in the season that the male redstarts molt into full black-and-orange plumage.

Before young white-crowneds get their distinct plumage, they sport brown-and-tan stripes.

WHITE-CROWNED SPARROW

Sometimes sparrows are affectionately called "little brown jobs." Their immature plumage makes them even more nondescript, but one species that stands out during immaturity is the white-crowned sparrow. The bold nutmeg brown stripes on top of its head are a good field mark. These birds typically turn black and white the following spring, when the bird is almost a year old.

A fledgling cardinal (left) typically appears disheveled, but even more so when enjoying a bath with its mom.

NORTHERN CARDINAL

Adolescent northern cardinals always look as if they have bed head because of a thin wispy crest of feathers. They also have nearly black beaks, which lighten up as the summer progresses and, come autumn, have the characteristic red-orange bill of the species. By then, a few scarlet body feathers are observable on young males, too, but until that time, both sexes appear similar to adult females with light coloring.

A male northern cardinal feeds his offspring.

It may take almost a full year for an immature red-headed woodpecker to grow all of its red feathers.

RED-HEADED WOODPECKER

Many woodpeckers have red coloring on their heads, but one of the few with an entirely red head is, you guessed it, the red-headed woodpecker. Confusingly, the juvenile has a brown head and heavy brown markings that break up the rest of its pattern. Watch for broad flashes of white across the wings, lower back and rump, contrasting with the darker upper back, wing tips and tail. By fall, some red feathers may appear on the head, but many brown feathers may be retained in the next year.

Young Bird Basics

These telltale signs separate the kids from the grown-ups.

- Juveniles often have a soft, fluffy look, even beyond the down feather nestling stage.

- A fleshy gape—the area where the upper and lower bills connect—is a hint you're looking at an immature bird.

- After they leave the nest, they still exhibit food-begging behavior. However, in some species, this is also a courtship ritual of adults.

- Like toddlers learning to walk, growing birds can be awkward in flight. Landings are known to be especially tricky.

- Young birds may seem helpless, but they're tougher than you think. It's best to give them their space and let them be.

SEEING

Western
meadowlark

DOUBLE

Eastern
meadowlark

*For many popular
eastern birds,
there's a look-alike
in the west.*

By Ken Keffer

Western
bluebird

Eastern
bluebird

W

hether it's the eastern or the western version, orioles and bluebirds are favorites from coast to coast. And if you happen to be in the Great Plains, where many of their ranges overlap, there are twice as many iconic birds for you to observe.

Some of the species separations came about during a glacial period. Other genetic shifts happened earlier. Whatever the cause, these changes challenge us to compare eastern and western birdlife.

Baltimore and Bullock's Orioles

Formerly one species, the northern oriole is now known in the east as the Baltimore oriole and in the west as Bullock's oriole. Males of both species are brilliant orange and readily feed from orange halves, enjoy grape jelly and occasionally taste hummingbird nectar. An adult male Baltimore has a fully black head, but the head of the Bullock's is only partially black, among other subtle differences.

Orioles of the Americas are named after a family of birds from Europe and Asia. They aren't truly related to their namesakes, however. Instead, the North American orioles are in the same family as blackbirds, cowbirds and meadowlarks.

Eastern and Western Bluebirds

A whole slew of birds include "eastern" and "western" in their names, among them bluebirds. The easiest way to tell the two bluebirds apart is geography. If you happen to find yourself looking at a bluebird in West Texas during the winter or in southeastern Arizona, though, you'll have to put a little more thought into your identification, because it could be either one.

Eastern bluebirds have reddish-brown feathers under the bill, but western bluebirds have blue or gray throats. The belly colors can be helpful, because eastern bluebirds have white ones, and those in the west have more dingy, gray bellies.

Bullock's
oriole

Baltimore
oriole

Indigo
bunting

Lazuli
bunting

Male lazuli and indigo
buntings are easy to tell apart,
but notice how they both have
the classic bunting bill.

Spotted
towhee

Eastern
towhee

Eastern
screech-owl

Western
screech-owl

THIS PAGE LEFT: RAY COLEMAN/DAVID LIEBMAN; RIGHT: ALL CANADA PHOTOS/

Mountain bluebirds, also of the west, are all blue and have none of the reddish-orange coloring seen on both eastern and western bluebirds.

Eastern and Spotted Towhees

Older field guides show the rufous-sided towhee as a single widespread species. Researchers split the species into eastern and spotted in 1995. Like many eastern and western pairs, the towhees hybridize with each other in the Great Plains, where their ranges overlap.

Most towhees have red eyes and a combination of black, white and reddish coloring. Spotted towhees have white dots on their backs and wings instead of solid colors. Scientists speculate that the spots replicate dappled sunlight in the dry thickets where spotted towhees are often found in the West.

Indigo and Lazuli Buntings

This pairing is one of the easiest to tell apart, at least when it comes to the males. Male indigos are fully blue, while male lazulis are patterned blue on the top, with an orange breast, white wing bars and white along the belly. The females of both species are a uniform brown with a slight blue hue. These two bunting species also have one of the most extensive hybridization zones, stretching from southern Saskatchewan to Arizona.

Both buntings are found in shrubby edges and open areas. They occasionally make an appearance at bird feeders, and both species are sure to dazzle anyone who is lucky enough to spot one in their backyard.

Eastern and Western Meadowlarks

Perhaps one of the hardest duos to tell apart are eastern and western meadowlarks, which have extensive overlapping ranges. Curiously, the two species rarely hybridize with one another. The easiest way to sort out eastern from western meadowlarks is by voice, which is how the birds tell themselves apart, too! Eastern meadowlarks have a simpler, high-pitched song. Their western counterparts sing with complex whistles and warbles.

Both meadowlarks can be found as far southwest as Arizona and New Mexico. The overlapping ranges continue northeast across the Plains all the way to the western Great Lakes states and Ontario.

Eastern and Western Screech-Owls

These smallish owls, only about 8 inches long, are remarkably similar. Easterns can be reddish, grayish or somewhere in between, while westerns are almost always gray. The western screech-owl's voice has a bouncing-ball sound, whereas the eastern screech-owl performs whinnies and trills.

The ranges of these two species overlap slightly in the Western plains, but for the most part, western screech-owls range from West Texas to British Columbia, while eastern screech-owls are found east of the Rockies.

INTO THE *Woods!*

Go beyond the backyard to see warblers, the bright and colorful stars of spring migration. **By Kirsten Sweet**

Common yellowthroat

It's worth a visit to a marshy area for a quick look at common yellowthroats. Although they try to remain out of sight, they flit in and out of reeds and cattails. Listen for the *wichity-wichity-wichity* song, and look for the male's distinct black mask.

American redstart

Bright yellow plumage is common among warblers. But the male American redstart, covered in mostly black, breaks all the rules. Redstarts are among the most active warblers, showing off orange-red patches as they flit through trees. Be on the lookout for redstarts if you're birding on Eastern forest edges.

Magnolia warbler

This easy-to-spot warbler spends time in low shrubs and small trees. During spring migration, magnolia warblers zip through the eastern half of the U.S. on the way to their breeding grounds in Canada and in northern states like Minnesota and Wisconsin.

Hooded warbler

Unlike many warblers, this species forages, and even nests, close to the ground. The male's black hood around a yellow face helps with ID when he's spotted in his ideal habitat—shady under-growth in the Southeast and Northeast during summer breeding season.

Yellow warbler

It's hard to miss the brilliantly colored yellow warbler. One of the most common of the 50 warbler species, you won't have to go deep into the forest to see one. Yellows can be found near open woods, streams, orchards and even roadsides.

Black-throated blue warbler

The male's dark colors reflect this bird's favorite migration habitat: in the shadows of undergrowth in Eastern woods. The females look completely different, with dull olive coloring.

Chestnut-sided warbler

No other warbler sports such a unique color combination. An olive-yellow cap and rufous sides make the chestnut-sided a showstopper. It passes through the eastern U.S. during migration, so be on the lookout for this beauty on forest edges.

Yellow-throated warbler

The vibrant yellow throat is an important field mark of this species. These warblers are early migrants and spend their summers in the southeastern U.S. They forage high in the canopy of swamp and pine forests.

Prairie warbler

Don't let the name fool you! These streaky-faced birds prefer dense thickets throughout the eastern U.S. Males have signature chestnut-colored marks on their backs. Females have similar, though subtler, markings.

Black-throated green warbler

Listen for the male's recognizable song, *zoo, zee, zoo zoo zee*, and then look up—way up! These birds stay high in coniferous or mixed forests throughout summer in the Northeast. They are "green" because both males and females have olive backs.

MOLTING MASTERS OF

In the fall, male American goldfinches lose their brilliant yellow feathers, and new brown ones grow in instead. This process is called molting.

DISGUISE

Now you see them, now you don't! Discover why birds change color in the fall and how to identify them.
By Kenn and Kimberly Kaufman

MALE SCARLET
TANAGERS
change from
red and black to
dull yellow (right)
in late summer.

As summer slips into fall and the weather cools down, swimsuits and shorts are swapped for sweaters and scarves. Birds also change their wardrobes with the seasons. Many species look the same 365 days of the year, but some look so different in fall that they are challenging to identify.

DISAPPEARING ACT

Take the American goldfinch, for example. All summer, glowing yellow male American goldfinches nibble at your feeder, and then one fall day there's not a bright lemon-colored songbird to be found. In fact, the goldfinches are still around and coming to feeders. They just look different—drab and dull. The color changes of the female American goldfinch are subtle, but the male is all drama. He transitions from blazing yellow to a much duller yellow-brown, making him look more like the female.

His feathers aren't actually changing color. Instead, the bird gradually replaces all the feathers in a process called molting. Over the span of a few weeks, old feathers slowly drop out and new ones grow in. If you spot the male goldfinch in the middle of molting, he'll have patches of yellow and brown. But once he's decked out in his autumn garb, you'd never guess he was once bright yellow.

PRESTO CHANGE-O

Molting isn't unique to goldfinches. As a rule, any healthy wild songbird replaces its feathers at least once a year. Late summer to fall is the most common time for this to happen, but in many cases it's not too noticeable. A male cardinal, for example, replaces old red feathers with new red feathers, so he looks freshened up but otherwise unchanged. It's another story, of course, when birds molt into a completely different plumage in fall.

One bird that changes in a big way is the male scarlet tanager, which is scarlet for only half the year. In late summer, this species replaces all its feathers before migrating to South America in fall. The male plumage changes from brilliant red to dull yellowish-green, like the female's. The same thing happens to the bobolink of meadows and hayfields. The male bobolink's breeding plumage of black, yellow and white is replaced by a yellowish-brown sparrowlike pattern before he flies off to South America in fall. The male indigo bunting goes from an intense deep blue in spring and summer to mostly brown.

FLEDGLING FEATS

A new challenge in late summer comes as young birds leave the nest, looking very different from their parents. Baby chipping sparrows are covered with dark streaks, while their parents have smooth gray chests and reddish caps. Fledgling robins and bluebirds are covered with spots at first but eventually lose them as they grow up. The majority of small birds, however,

Young cedar waxwings (top) and adults sport yellow bands on their tails. Use that clue to identify tricky juveniles in fall.

molt their body and head feathers soon after they become independent, quickly replacing their juvenile plumage. Within a month, they look recognizably similar to adults.

Once fall arrives, some young birds look very different. Cedar waxwings usually nest late in summer, so you might see streaky brown juveniles as late as November. Young red-headed woodpeckers have brown heads until late fall and occasionally through the winter. And while adult white-crowned sparrows are smooth gray and brown with sharp black-and-white head stripes, their kids have brown-and-tan stripes on their heads through their first fall and winter.

CRACK THE CODE

The good news is that as tough as it can be to identify adults that change color or youngsters that look different from their parents, it's not impossible. For starters, when you see an odd bird in fall, look beyond its colors and focus on its shape, size and actions. Even without bright hues, a male scarlet tanager is still a medium-size songbird with a thick bill that moves quietly through the foliage in tall trees. Although a young cedar waxwing has stripes on its chest, it's still a crested bird that sits upright, eats berries and flies out to catch insects in midair. It's also likely to be in a flock with other waxwings.

Another tried-and-true tip is to look closely at the wings and tail. On most birds, these don't change as much as the head and body do. That male scarlet tanager may be mostly greenish-yellow in autumn, but he still has black wings. The young cedar waxwing has a yellow band at the tip of its tail, just like the adults.

A good way to practice fall bird ID skills is to look at those American goldfinches again. The males lose their bold color, but they're still tiny birds with thick, seed-crunching beaks. They're still active and sociable, moving around in flocks, with a bouncy flight and short musical calls. They still have black wings with white or buff wing bars, and white spots on black tails. The bright gold color may be gone, but that goldfinch personality is always present.

Soon it'll be spring again. Watch your feeders, and you may witness a magical transformation as the goldfinches go from patchy brown and yellow on the way to a sparkling summer wardrobe.

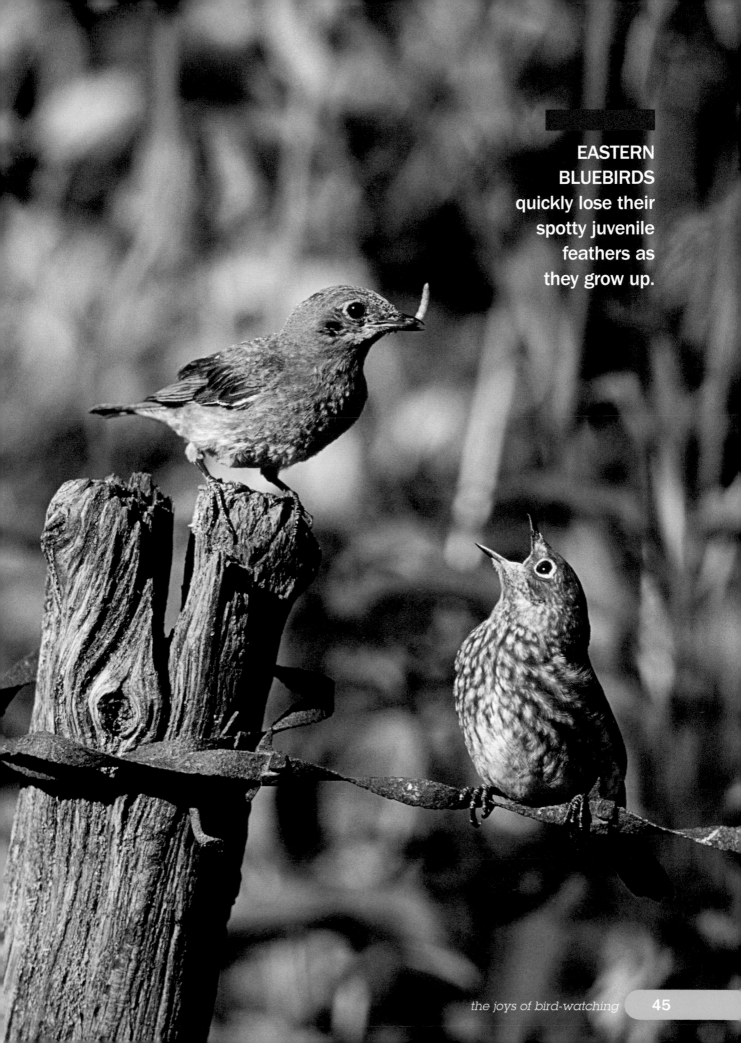

EASTERN BLUEBIRDS quickly lose their spotty juvenile feathers as they grow up.

FANCY

WALK THIS WAY AND LEARN WHY FEET ARE AS IMPORTANT AS FEATHERS. By Kenn and Kimberly Kaufman

FOOTWORK

AS BIRD LOVERS, we spend a lot of time in awe of birds for their brightly patterned plumage, wing shapes and entertaining antics, not to mention that they can *fly*. But when not soaring through the sky, birds rely on their specially structured feet to get around. Their unique toes come in arrangements such as zygodactyl and anisodactyl, which may sound more like the names of their distant dinosaur cousins—but don't worry! You can still appreciate just how crucial birds' feet really are. No scientific memorization required.

Check out those long toes! Because of this foot structure, green herons can walk in soft sand and wet mud.

FEET FOR PERCHING

Many backyard birds, from robins to wrens and phoebes to finches, belong to a large group called perching birds. The structure of their feet helps them perch on thin twigs. These birds have three toes pointing forward and one pointing backward, an anisodactyl arrangement, so each foot touches the perch at four separate points. When birds settle on a twig, their toes automatically tighten, thanks to the muscles in the legs and feet. Similarly, when birds rise up, the toes loosen their grip. Chickadees that flit from branch to branch may grasp and release different perches thousands of times a day.

FEET FOR WALKING

Wild turkeys and ring-necked pheasants walk more than fly and have strong, sturdy legs and toes. Males of both species have a spur on the back of the leg, which they may use when they get into fights. It's typical for birds that spend a lot of time on the ground, especially hard ground, to have strong feet.

Another bird known for strong legs is the greater roadrunner of the desert Southwest. This bird has zygodactyl feet (two toes pointing forward and two backward). It leaves X-shaped tracks, and Native American legends celebrated the fact that no one could tell from the tracks which way the bird was going. True to its name, the roadrunner can run at 20 miles per hour for quite a distance.

The ultimate walking bird is probably the ostrich, the tallest bird in the world. Its small wings are useless for flight, but it has huge, muscular legs and feet. While most birds have four toes and a few have three, ostriches are the only birds in the world with only two toes on each foot.

FEET FOR SWIMMING

Birds that swim have special requirements. They paddle with their feet to move across the water's surface, but the skinny little toes of a typical bird wouldn't be useful for pushing against water. However, with webbing stretched between the toes, those feet become very effective fins. The webbed feet of ducks, geese and swans are widely known, but we also see webbed feet on many unrelated waterbirds, such as pelicans, loons and gulls.

Some waterbirds have only partial webbing, often in the form of expanded lobes or flaps along the edges of the toes. The bizarre feet of the American coot offer an interesting example. Those lobed toes are good for swimming, and they're also suited for walking on land. However, grebes rarely come out on land, and they also have lobed toes.

FEET FOR UNEVEN SURFACES

Birds can't walk on water, but some marsh birds come close, with long toes that allow them to traipse across the surface of very wet mud or floating plants. We see this long-toed shape on various herons, rails and sandpipers. The extreme examples are found on tropical shorebirds called jacanas. Their ridiculously long toes allow jacanas to walk around easily on top of floating

TINTED TOES

Bird feet tend to have dull, dark colors, but here are a few that flaunt bright hues.

1. **Snowy egret:**
   Black legs and yellow feet
2. **Blue-footed booby:**
   You can guess this one!
3. **Least bittern:**
   Greenish-yellow legs and feet
4. **Louisiana waterthrush:**
   Bubblegum pink feet
5. **Blackpoll warbler:**
   Yellow feet
6. **Horned puffin:** Orange feet
7. **White ibis:** Red legs and feet

Brown-headed nuthatches' feet help them acrobatically cling to perches.

Woodpeckers, nuthatches and creepers are tree-climbers. Their powerful gripping toes help them cling to bark or dead wood.

Red-bellied woodpecker

Strong legs allow greater roadrunners to run 20 miles per hour.

lily pads—in fact, "lily-trotter" is one nickname for them. One species, the northern jacana, shows up in southern Texas at times.

What about walking on frozen water? Ptarmigan are small grouse that live in the far North and high mountains, regions covered with deep snow for much of the year. Like other grouse, they have fairly short toes. But ptarmigan grow a fringe of stiff feathers along the sides of their toes; the stiff feathers act like snowshoes, allowing these birds to walk across the surface of soft, fluffy snow.

FEET FOR FEEDING

The word "raptor" comes from a root word that means "to seize and carry away." Hawks, falcons and owls have strong toes and long, sharp, curved claws specialized for hunting, capturing and carrying prey. Most birds use their feet for sitting in one place or moving around, but for these birds of prey, their feet are their essential tools.

Most hawks and falcons have three forward toes and one back toe. On owls, however, the outer toe is reversible: It usually swivels to the back when the owl is perched or grasping prey, giving it a zygodactyl arrangement with two toes forward and two back, but sometimes it perches with three toes forward. And then there's the osprey, which also has this reversible outer toe. The osprey, or fish hawk, is famous for diving feetfirst into water to catch fish. Besides being able to swivel its outer toe around, the osprey also has very rough scales on the soles of its toes, which likely help it keep a firm grip on slippery fish.

Raptors are big enough that you can easily see their claws, but the structure and look of songbirds' feet is often overlooked. Head outside and observe how even the most common birds in your backyard get around when they're not flying. It's proof that from their feathers to their toes, birds are endlessly fascinating.

glad you asked!

Kenn and Kimberly Kaufman answer your birding questions.

Q&A

What can I do to attract a Carolina wren pair to my nest box?

Gwen Falkenstein CARLISLE, PENNSYLVANIA

Kenn and Kimberly: Carolina wrens have been known to nest in tin cans, boots, mailboxes, even a pocket of blue jeans hanging on a clothesline! But while they're willing to nest in unconventional structures, they can be picky about the area where they're willing to build. Carolina wrens prefer bushy habitat with lots of cover. If possible, allow an area on your property to become a bit more wild and unruly, and place a wren box near that area. You might also offer a supply of nest materials such as feathers, moss and small twigs to add more incentive.

Barred owls sometimes call and even hunt during the daytime.

Why would crows chase an owl? I have seen four or five crows flying after and around a barred owl, cawing and squawking, on several occasions.

Mary Leffler REYNOLDSBURG, OHIO

Kenn and Kimberly: Many kinds of birds will harass owls that they discover in the daytime, in a behavior called "mobbing." Even chickadees will mob little screech-owls. Crows focus on bigger targets like barred owls or great horned owls, and they will also chase hawks and eagles. No one has come up with a complete explanation for why they do this. It may serve to draw attention to these predators so they can't take smaller birds by surprise. In the case of the crows, which are intelligent and curious birds, it may be partly a tough-guy way of having fun!

BACKYARD TIP
In the Southwest, plant native shrubs to attract verdins for nesting and roosting, and to provide shade for them during hot summers.

Verdins are adorable, with their yellow heads and friendly demeanor. How can I bring verdins to my yard?

Diane Pelinga LAS VEGAS, NEVADA

Kenn and Kimberly: We agree, the verdin is a very appealing little bird! This resident of the desert Southwest likes open habitats, and it will readily come into yards that have a few native trees and shrubs such as mesquites, acacias or palo verdes. It feeds mostly on insects, so it's not attracted to birdseed; but it also likes nectar, so a garden with native flowering plants may draw it in. The verdin is also a frequent visitor to hummingbird feeders. Since you might see hummingbirds at any season around Las Vegas, put up some sugar-water feeders and you may also attract verdins.

I purchased a heated birdbath and am disappointed in the amount of birds that have visited it. What's the problem? Do birds get water from snow or could my bath be too close to the house?

Randy Childers
FAIRMONT, MINNESOTA

Kenn and Kimberly: Some birds do eat snow, so they may not have to visit baths to drink water very often. They'll stay longer if they're bathing, but birds can be fussy about using birdbaths. Often, the basin of the bath is simply too deep. If your birdbath has a basin that's more than an inch or so deep, adjust the depth by adding a layer of pea gravel to the bottom. The gravel makes it shallower and provides a nice surface for the birds to stand on while they bathe. If you don't think depth is the issue, your birdbath might indeed be too close to the house.

A few of these birds visited my feeders in early February. Were they just passing through?

Diane White NORTH STREET, MICHIGAN

Kenn and Kimberly: This is a male white-winged crossbill, a bird that isn't a common visitor to feeders. Crossbills show up frequently in Michigan, but they don't stay there—in fact, they don't stay anywhere. These are great nomads, wandering throughout the evergreen forests of Alaska, Canada and the northern states, migrating at almost any season and settling down to nest and raise young when they find an abundant crop of spruce cones. When the crossbills left your yard, they might have gone in any direction. You may see them again, but they're so unpredictable that we can't guess when they might arrive!

BACKYARD TIP
Attract nesting bluebirds with a nest box placed about 3 to 6 feet high in an open area.

A male northern cardinal loves our hanging suet. We thought cardinals were ground feeders. Is this normal?

Bill Roberts HUDSON, NEW HAMPSHIRE

Kenn and Kimberly: While dangling cardinals aren't all that common, we do see this happen from time to time. There are several possible explanations. Cardinals show a strong affinity for sunflower and safflower seeds. If your suet has seeds mixed in, it could be enough for your cardinal to turn into a daredevil. Some individual birds also have a more adventurous streak, and this cardinal may have tried the suet after watching other birds feed that way. It might also be happening because of the time of year, since birds have an instinct to consume more protein during the breeding season.

DID YOU KNOW?
Cardinals aren't picky. They eat fruit, seeds, peanuts, corn, insects and even suet.

Our bluebird house had eggs and babies for many years. One year, there were four eggs to start, and then three were gone and the fourth had been opened. What happened?

Pauline Kelly HOMEWOOD, ALABAMA

Kenn and Kimberly: This sounds like the work of a house wren. While small and cute, house wrens can be hostile during nesting season. If they set up house in your yard and encounter other cavity nesters they deem too close for comfort, they'll pierce the eggs of other species and carry them off. So we have to learn to love them in spite of their behavior. The best way to protect your bluebirds is to make sure the nest box is a fair distance away from the dense cover preferred by house wrens and to install another box a good distance away from your existing box.

Bird Anatomy 101

Prepare to be impressed as you take a closer look at your backyard visitors.
By David Mizejewski

We all enjoy seeing birds in our gardens. But if you asked the average person to describe a bird, the answer probably would be a quick overview of its feathers and beak, perhaps with a short imitation of its call.

When you truly look closely at a bird, though, you'll see that these creatures have a fascinating anatomy unique in nature.

Let's consider three key areas.

FEATHERS

The most noticeable feature of bird anatomy is the feather. No other living group of animals on the planet has them (although some extinct ones did). And as much as feathers may resemble one another superficially, they're all different. Owls, for instance, have large flight feathers with a delicate fringe along the outer edge that allows for completely silent flight.

But there's more to feathers than flight. After all, not all birds fly, but they all have feathers. In fact, feathers most likely first evolved as a means of insulation and protection from the elements, like hair in mammals.

Birds use their feathers for communication. Males of many species sport brightly colored or ornate ones as a way to woo females. And most species can puff up their feathers to intimidate rivals or predators.

BEAKS

Whether you prefer to say beaks or bills, these are as varied as feathers. Each is adapted to the kinds of food a bird species eats. Cardinals and grosbeaks have heavy, blunt beaks designed to crush the shells of seeds and nuts. Robins, mockingbirds and catbirds have narrow, pointed beaks for plucking berries and catching insects. Mourning doves, quail and sparrows have short beaks for picking tiny seeds. Hawks have sharp, curved beaks for eating meat, while hummingbirds have long, narrow beaks in order to reach into tubular flowers for sweet nectar.

Birds also use their beaks to fend off attacks.

FEET

The bird world has a surprising diversity of feet, each shape suited to the species' survival. Ducks and other waterfowl have webbed feet to propel them through the water. Birds of prey are armed with sharp, hooked talons for catching and killing. Wading birds, such as herons, have wide feet to support them on sticky mud so they don't sink. Songbirds have delicate, grasping feet for clutching the tree branches where they perch. Woodpeckers and their relatives have zygodactyl feet—with two toes pointing forward and two backward—which allow them to cling to and move up and down tree trunks.

No matter what shape, size or color of the various features of a bird's anatomy, one thing is true: They all help birds survive. The next time you're watching birds in your yard, take a minute to notice their anatomical features and to marvel at the beautiful symbiosis that every bird species has with its environment.

bird dinosaurs

Not all dinosaurs went extinct—one branch of these ancient reptiles evolved into birds. We know this because modern birds share anatomical features with a group of small, carnivorous dinosaurs. They have the same kind of respiratory system, many of the same skeletal structures and, yes, even feathers. Look at an ostrich or a hawk, and it's not difficult to imagine a velociraptor, a dinosaur species that we now know was indeed feathered.

Sharp beak for
eating meat

Fringed wing
feathers for
silent flight

Talons for
gripping prey

A bird's anatomy is
adapted to its habitat
and behavior, as you
can see with this great
horned owl.

A tufted titmouse shows signs of albinism: pink legs and a pink bill.

Albinism in Birds

The answers behind the mysterious white-feathered bird in your backyard are revealed. By David Mizejewski

Observe birds coming and going through a backyard long enough, and eventually you'll spot one that has partially white or all-white feathers where there should be color. These birds have a genetic condition known as leucism or, more rarely, albinism, which affects their coloring as well as their ability to survive in the wild. The next time you spot one of these fascinating birds, you'll know if it's leucistic or albino.

ALBINISM

Birds that lack the color pigment melanin have a genetic mutation called albinism. These birds are often pure white, but in some cases an albino bird might still have yellow or orange feathers. Those warmer colors are carotenoid pigments, rather than melanin ones, so they're still present in birds with albinism. The true test of whether a bird is an albino is in its eyes. The lack of melanin allows blood vessels to show through, causing their eyes to be bright pink or red.

On the other end of the color spectrum is a genetic condition called melanism, in which a bird has extra melanin pigmentation. These birds appear darker than the typical coloration for their species.

LEUCISM

Often confused with albinism is a lesser-known genetic condition called leucism, in which not just melanin but other color pigments are reduced as well. Unlike albinism, leucism doesn't completely eliminate pigment. Leucistic birds appear lighter than normal but aren't fully white. Sometimes these birds are pale, with an overall lightening of their coloring. In other cases, leucism can result in a bird being pied or piebald—with white patches across its body. Because they don't fully lack melanin, leucistic birds have normal-colored eyes rather than the pink or red eyes of albinos.

Despite her lack of blue coloring, this female eastern bluebird found a mate.

The white patches covering this American robin are a hint that it is leucistic, not albino.

ALBINISM IMPACT

Compared to typically colored members of their species, albino birds are at a great disadvantage. The white feathers stand out against vegetation; thus, without camouflage, albino birds are easier for predators to spot. Their feathers do offer some protection in snow, but unfortunately they reduce a bird's ability to retain heat. Dark colors absorb heat, light colors reflect it, which can mean life or death in freezing temperatures.

Birds with albinism suffer from weak feathers due to a lack of melanin. Their feathers break and deteriorate over time. Albino birds also have poor eyesight—another hindrance. As a result, these birds rarely survive past fledging.

Leucistic birds have slightly better chances because they retain some pigmentation. That means the light-colored bird you see in your yard is more likely leucistic than albino.

Either way, it's a rare and exciting sight when such a unique bird stops for a visit!

Look at the pink bill on this albino or leucistic hummingbird.

5 facts about discoloration

• Genetics determine true albino birds: Both parents have to carry the uncommon recessive genes that produce rare pure-white offspring.

• A pied or piebald bird's leucistic feathers are rarely in a symmetrical pattern.

• Typically, leucism affects only dark feathers, so some birds with leucism have white feathers while still maintaining the bright colors of their red, orange or yellow feathers.

• A bird is a true albino if its feet, legs, bill and eyes are pale pink or red.

• Birds with discoloration may struggle during courtship. Many birds use plumage color as a way to find and recognize potential mates.

FLYING

UNDER THE RADAR

Keep your eyes peeled for flycatchers. These unsung birds deserve a little time in the spotlight. By David Shaw

Look for scissor-tailed flycatchers if you live in or are passing through the south-central United States.

ROLF NUSSBAUMER

I was clad in chest waders, it was hot and the mosquitoes were out in full force. I had been walking for miles in up to a foot of water atop slippery trails and tree roots. Not an ideal day on the job, but it's the cost of field biology in the remote boreal forest of Alaska.

Olive-sided flycatchers sing from the tops of tall snags in boreal and coniferous forests.

I concentrated on the bright songs of birds. Yet as I splashed through another long stretch of saturated trail, the idea of a desk job didn't seem all that bad.

Then I heard the distant but still loud three-note whistle I'd been hoping to hear. A year earlier, an olive-sided flycatcher had been captured, banded and equipped with a tiny data collector near the spot where I was walking. My job was to see if it had come back.

As I approached, the unmistakable *quick! three-beers!* song erupted from a far-off stand of white spruces. Finally I spotted the bird through my binoculars as it perched at the very top of a spruce, head raised in song. It had returned!

This olive-sided flycatcher had arrived from its wintering grounds in the Amazon rain forest. I've spent time in the jungles of South America, and the place seemed so far removed from the spruce forests of the subarctic that it was almost too much to believe. When I captured the bird two days later and removed the tiny geolocator from its back, the data proved it.

Birds in the flycatcher group are often overlooked. Many appear so frustratingly similar to one another (various mixes of olive green, white and gray) that many casual birders simply ignore them. Even their songs—combinations of squeaky, nasal notes—lack excitement. They are suboscine songbirds, which means that, unlike thrushes, wrens and warblers, they lack the necessary anatomy for elaborate song. But there is far more to flycatchers than meets the eye (or ear). Some are by no means dull in appearance, and even those that are plain make up for their lack of flash through staggering migrations. Like the olive-sided species that flies to Alaska, they are too interesting to ignore. Here are a few favorites.

Watch for drab-looking alder flycatchers this fall as they pass through the eastern U.S.

ALDER

The alder flycatcher is a member of the genus *Empidonax*, which may be the most difficult group of songbirds to separate into species. Like many of its sister species, the alder is small and olive green, with a pale breast and a partial eye ring. Its song is a lackluster, nasal two-note call. But this songbird, weighing about half an ounce, makes an astonishing yearly migration, traversing the entire Western Hemisphere from its breeding grounds in the boreal forest of Alaska and Canada to the chilly temperate climate of the western Amazon rain forest. Few songbirds complete a migration of that scale.

SCISSOR-TAILED

Flashes of pink set off the scissor-tail's pale gray and black plumage, and its ludicrously long tail, as the name implies, scissors back and forth when the bird moves. A migrant like most flycatchers, this lovely bird spends summers in the southern Great Plains. In winter, scissor-taileds move south into Central America.

There, they occupy a similar open-fields habitat, in which they flutter from low perches to snatch insects in the air.

VERMILION

Unabashedly flashy, the male vermilion flycatcher is bright crimson with black wings and brows. Once you lay eyes on a male, you won't forget him. My first was in Baja California—a male perched on a lower frond of a date palm over a quiet pool. Looking like a wildly out-of-place Christmas bauble, he sallied out, snatched a damselfly from the air, returned to his perch, delicately plucked the wings from the insect and swallowed the rest. In general, the vermilion is migratory only at the northern extent of its breeding range in the south-central and southwest United States. Through most of its range in Mexico and Central and South America, it's a year-round resident.

GREAT CRESTED

This large bird belongs to a second frustrating-for-birders genus, *Myiarchus*. Many of the look-alike species of this

Great cresteds are the only flycatchers in eastern North America that nest in tree cavities.

group are restricted to the tropics of Central and South America, but the great crested flycatcher makes its summer home across the eastern half of the U.S. Though not as dashing as the vermilion or scissor-tailed, this species manages a bit of flash in the form of a lemon yellow abdomen and a splash of cinnamon red in the outer wing feathers. The birds have a fondness for open forests, where their buzzy single-note calls and whistles emerge from the canopy.

FLYCATCHER CHALLENGE

I love this group of birds, perhaps because it is so often overlooked. Many of the species present an identification challenge, and the unexpected flare of colors and plumages that appear on others is a nice surprise. And with their presence comes a hint of the warm tropics, where most spend their winters.

Find out which flycatchers are in your area, and see if you can locate and identify them. They're not typical feeder birds, so go on an adventure to a local park or wildlife refuge near you.

As scissor-tails fly, salmon pink colors flash under the wings as the long tail scissors back and forth.

SEE THESE SPECIES!
Because almost all of North America's flycatchers are migratory—and many more live just south of the border—there's no better place to find them than the southern tip of Texas. Hundreds of migrating and breeding birds, including about 20 flycatcher species, can be seen at Laguna Atascosa National Wildlife Refuge.

Get to Know Grosbeaks

Look for these large, eye-catching birds.

DID YOU KNOW?
Where their ranges overlap, rose-breasted grosbeaks, like this one, sometimes breed with a close relative, black-headed grosbeaks.

Blue grosbeak

Pine grosbeak

Evening grosbeak

What's in a Name?

All grosbeaks—rose-breasted, blue, black-headed, pine and evening grosbeaks—share a common characteristic: a thick, conical bill for cracking tough seeds. Although these species go by the same descriptive name, grosbeak, they belong to different families. Pine and evening grosbeaks are finches; the others are in the cardinal family.

Eastern Favorite

Rose-breasted grosbeaks are a welcome sign of spring in the eastern U.S. These birds prefer a leafy, wooded habitat but also show up at backyard feeders. They love sunflower seeds, but they'll eat raw peanuts and safflower seeds, too. The male rose-breasted is dapper with his bright red chest patch. The female is striped brown and white.

Southern Specialty

A telltale sign you're looking at a blue grosbeak is the cinnamon-colored wing bars. Found mainly in the South, blue grosbeaks look for shrubby habitats, such as old fields, forest edges and riversides. You might lure a blue grosbeak to a feeder with grains and seeds, as long as your backyard includes dense shrubbery. The male is bright blue and the female is light brown with rusty wing bars.

Western Favorite

Black-headed grosbeaks spend summers in mixed woodlands and riverside trees in the West. You might spot them sipping nectar from an oriole cup or cracking sunflower seeds at a main feeder. Male black-headed grosbeaks are dull orange-brown with a black head, while females are brown and white with orange tones.

Forest Dweller

At a whopping 9 inches, pine grosbeaks are big and a bit sluggish. They live in boreal coniferous forests of the far North and high mountains of the West, but a few wander into the northeastern U.S. in winter. If you're lucky enough to attract a pine grosbeak to your feeder, take note of the male's pink coloring. Females and young males are gray with touches of yellow or orange.

Winter Wanderer

There's no telling when or where evening grosbeaks, with their spectacular gold and dusky coloring, will show up. Winter migrants, they spend the season searching for food, typically tree seeds. They sometimes visit backyards for sunflower seeds at feeders or to nibble at trees with berries or buds, especially maples.

BACKYARD TIPS
Field editors share their grosbeak success stories.

Rose-breasted grosbeaks visit my feeders as they migrate north in spring. They seem to enjoy the same seeds as the cardinals—a mix with mostly black oil sunflower seeds—and they prefer tray feeders.
Boni Trombetta
WEST CHESTER, PENNSYLVANIA

Black-headed grosbeak

Black-headed grosbeaks and their offspring frequent our feeders from early spring to early fall at our New Mexico mountain cabin. They are quite clownish as they line up on the deck railing awaiting "table" space at the feeders. This year we switched from a seed mix to only black oil sunflower seeds, and they still feed in large numbers.
Pat Northington
AUSTIN, TEXAS

bird tales

Readers share some of their best birding stories.

DID YOU KNOW?
Crabapples provide year-round interest for birds. Try to avoid the cultivars prone to disease.

I was surprised when this Baltimore oriole landed in my crabapple tree instead of at the grape jelly feeder, but I love how the white blooms are a striking contrast to the oriole's beautiful orange chest. Who knew I would attract so many colorful birds to our Indiana yard with this crabapple tree?
John Roberts WARSAW, INDIANA

We've been enjoying

a recent warm spell, and it reminded me of this moment I once captured in our backyard with a yellow warbler.

Ted Busby
CARLETON PLACE, ONTARIO

This indigo bunting

was a spring visitor last year. I was fortunate enough to capture this picture of him sitting on a thorny rosebush in our backyard perennial garden. He was like a flower among the thorns.

David Nehls IONIA, IOWA

A northern cardinal stopped by our Kanzan cherry tree last spring. It was such a stunning sight to look out of my kitchen window to see a bright red bird among lush pink cherry blossoms. I looked twice to make sure of what I saw. The cardinal stayed perfectly still long enough for me to capture the splendor.

Lesley Jeal
MANCHESTER, MICHIGAN

DID YOU KNOW?
To keep clean, hummingbirds preen their feathers after a bath or a visit to a mister.

At the start of migration, I noticed an influx of male hummingbirds, but I had put off photographing them because of the heat and humidity of central Alabama. A day dawned that was cooler but rainy. Overcast weather isn't the best for photographing hummingbirds, but I went outside anyway. The clouds broke just enough for overhead light, and the hummers were going crazy. I spent several hours with this particular male ruby-throated hummingbird. I like this shot because it's an unusual glimpse into the secret life of hummingbirds.

Julia Bartosh NOTASULGA, ALABAMA

For whatever reason, this oriole would take only the white yarn. When the white was gone, it quit coming. We put more white yarn out and it was back!

Roger Parsons
MIFFLINTOWN, PENNSYLVANIA

Who doesn't love a black-capped chickadee? This little bird was so calm and allowed me to get quite close while it enjoyed sniffing the flowers on my back porch. I love the specks of pollen on its face.

Steph DeFerie
HARWICH, MASSACHUSETTS

One early spring morning, I noticed this Canada goose with her goslings sleeping comfortably underneath her wing. It was a particularly cool morning and her little ones needed warmth. I quickly grabbed my camera, hoping they wouldn't move a feather until I had a chance to capture the moment. I was thrilled to see mom and babies still snuggled in as I snapped this photo. I never knew Canada geese did this—so adorable!

Joanne Killmer RINDGE, NEW HAMPSHIRE

Every morning, I put an orange half at my feeder for this female Bullock's oriole that nested near my home. I got a big kick out of her pose! She stood like this multiple times, and I thought she was trying to tell the other birds that the orange was hers.

Dawn Key ELIZABETH, COLORADO

BEACH BUM
Reddish egrets are rarely seen away from the coast. They love the salty waters of the Southeast.

I took this photo of a reddish egret wading at Fort De Soto Park, close to St. Petersburg, Florida. For more than an hour, the egret energetically ran through the water and used the shade of its wings to reduce the glare as it speared fish. A storm was coming in off the Gulf, and I had to pull myself away from this fascinating scene.

Ruth Skinner SEMINOLE, FLORIDA

did you know?

How many of these extinct bird species have you heard of?

100

Passenger pigeons have been extinct for more than 100 years. At one time, huge flocks of these birds darkened the sky as they moved around eastern North America.

6

Only six dusky seaside sparrows, all male, were left in 1979. Pollution, pesticides and loss of marsh habitat caused the extinction of the species.

80

Great auks were hunted for their meat, feathers and eggs, leading to their extinction in the 1800s. Today, stuffed specimens of this bird are rare; only about 80 exist in museum collections around the world.

1

Only one parrot species was native to the U.S.—the Carolina parakeet. These birds were abundant in North America until farmers killed them in large numbers, contributing to their official extinction in 1939.

1932

Heath hens vanished in 1932. A subspecies of today's greater prairie-chicken, they were last seen at a reserve on Martha's Vineyard.

83

The great toothed diver (*Hesperornis regalis*) lived more than 83 million years ago. Flightless, it used its hind legs and lobed toes to swim, similar to grebes. It was about 5 feet long!

3

The ivory-billed woodpecker was the third-largest woodpecker in the world. It was believed to have gone extinct at least 50 years ago, but brief sightings were reported from Arkansas' Big Woods in 2004 and 2005.

Northern cardinal
Finalist in our
Backyard Photo Contest
Photo by Warren Spreng

Painted bunting
Photo by Larry Ditto/KAC Productions

American goldfinch
Photo by Steve and Dave Maslowski

Great gray owl
Finalist in our
Backyard Photo Contest
Photo by Kurt Frieders

Baltimore orioles
Photo by Michael Berg

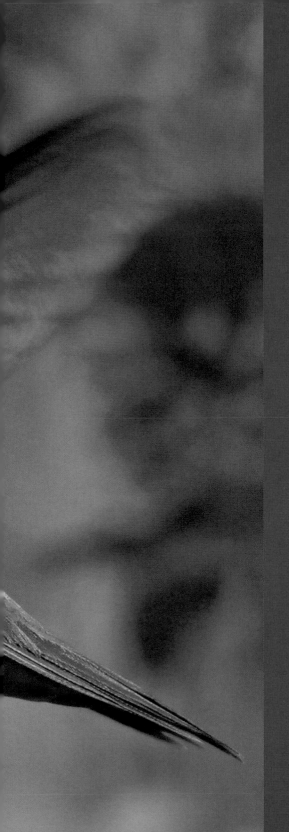

amazing
Hummingbirds

Enjoy gorgeous photos of these
adorable little birds, and learn about
some of their fascinating behaviors.
Find out what wildflowers attract
hummingbirds to your yard and how
to hand-feed the birds for a real thrill.

FRANCIS AND JANICE BERGQUIST

Female ruby-throated
hummingbird on tiger lilies by
Kristi Wenger Stoltzfus
STEELES TAVERN, VIRGINIA

hummingbirds

13

JAW-DROPPING FACTS
AND READER PHOTOS
THAT ARE BOUND TO
MAKE YOU ADORE THEM
EVEN MORE.

By Kirsten Sweet

1

While resting,
the average 4-inch
hummingbird takes
about 150 breaths
per minute.

2

A hummingbird uses its tongue, which functions as a tiny pump, to suck the sought-after sweet liquid from feeders and flowers.

Ruby-throated hummingbird by Carl Leichtenberger
PITTSFIELD, PENNSYLVANIA

3

Rufous hummingbirds migrate farther than any other North American species. They travel 4,000 miles from Mexico to Alaska every spring.

Rufous hummingbird by Robert Howson
KIRKLAND, WASHINGTON

Anna's hummingbird by
Desiree D. Skatvold
LIVERMORE, CALIFORNIA

4

The average nest is about the size of a half-dollar coin. The eggs inside the tiny structure look like mini white jelly beans.

5

Hummingbirds can be very territorial and will try to protect their food sources—both flowers and feeders. They spend a lot of time chasing other birds away.

Rufous hummingbirds by Rod Marr
ABBOTSFORD, BRITISH COLUMBIA

6

If you think the same hummingbirds come to your feeders and flowers every year, you might be right! Banding research shows they are likely to return to the area where they hatched.

Ruby-throated hummingbird by Gary Robinette
SPRINGFIELD, VIRGINIA

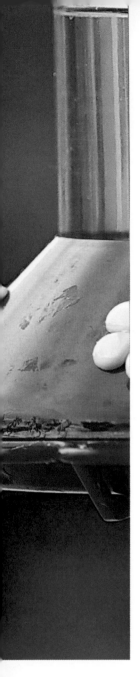

Juvenile ruby-throated
hummingbird by
Patty Jennings
STACYVILLE, MAINE

7

They can hover in
midair at flowers and
feeders, and they're the
only birds that can fly
backward. Their wings
move in a figure-eight
pattern, which allows
them to maneuver
with ease.

Ruby-throated
hummingbird by
Deb Forster
CLAYTON, NORTH CAROLINA

8 Some species, specifically male Anna's and Costa's,
are regular singers. Among other species, the most
common sounds are aggressive calls that resemble
chattering or squealing. You'll hear them when several
hummingbirds are gathered near a food source.

9

Rufous hummingbird by
Jeanette Brooks-Milano
CENTRALIA, WASHINGTON

Known for erratic movements, these agile birds beat their wings more than 50 times per second—even faster in extreme flight mode.

Ruby-throated
hummingbird by
Lonna Ours
PETERSBURG,
WEST VIRGINIA

10 Hummingbirds are solitary migrants, so you won't see them traveling in flocks. Wintering grounds vary by species, but most ruby-throats spend the cold months between southern Mexico and northern Panama.

11

You typically see hummingbirds at nectar blooms and sugar-water feeders, but they also eat tree sap and small insects when flowers are hard to find in the wild.

Costa's hummingbird by
Lisa J. Swanson
MARICOPA, ARIZONA

12

A birdbath with a small mister, bubbler or sprayer attracts hummingbirds. It's a rare sight, but they might fly through the mist of a lawn sprinkler, too!

13

Broad-tailed
hummingbird by
Jennifer Plunkett
ARVADA, COLORADO

It takes less than a week (about five to seven days) for a hummingbird to build its nest. Built by females only, nests are made of lichen, moss and spiderwebs.

Ruby-throated
hummingbird by
Tammi Elbert
WASHINGTON, MISSOURI

TOP 10
wildflowers for hummingbirds

Mimic a natural habitat with native blooms flowing with nectar. BY MELINDA MYERS

PICKING PLANTS
It's true: Hummingbirds love the color red. But they love it even more when it comes in the form of a tube-shaped bloom.

Rufous hummingbird at bee balm

TOP 10

1 COLUMBINE
2 SAGE
3 CARDINAL FLOWER
4 ANISE HYSSOP
5 BEE BALM
6 SCARLET GILIA
7 WOODLAND PHLOX
8 BEARDTONGUE
9 FRINGED BLEEDING HEART
10 LUPINE

If you're ready to create a hummingbird haven, start with colorful, showy wildflowers that are native to your area. These 10 plant picks will get you started. They perform well in a broad geographic range, bloom at different times and are relatively easy to find. Begin with these, then expand your garden with other native beauties that both you and the hummingbirds will love!

▲ Columbine

AQUILEGIA CANADENSIS, ZONES 3 TO 8

Bell-shaped red and yellow blooms emerge in spring and last until early summer. Grow columbine in full sun to partial shade and in well-draining soil. This wildflower, like many, seeds itself to create a colony of flowering plants for you to adore or share with others.

Why we love it: Hummingbirds love these plants, but deer and rabbits tend to leave columbine alone.

▲ Sage

SALVIA SPECIES, ZONES 3 TO 11, VARIES WITH SPECIES

There's a good chance you're already growing one or more of the 95 North American native salvias. With so many salvia options out there, you'll want to choose one that works in your zone. For example, mealycup salvia (*Salvia farinacea*) is a Texas native hardy in Zones 7 to 11 but grown as an annual elsewhere.

Why we love it: These plants, hummingbird magnets, come in several colors. Arizona sage has deep blue flowers, Texas sage has bright red flowers and Gregg's sage has white, pink or red flowers.

◀ Cardinal flower

LOBELIA CARDINALIS, ZONES 3 TO 9

Brighten up the summer garden with colorful spikes of scarlet red, white or rose flowers. Watch for butterflies that will also stop by for a visit, while the rabbits will usually pass on by. Add a few touches of blue to the garden with its close relative giant blue lobelia (*Lobelia siphilitica*).

Why we love it: Cardinal flowers are ideal for challenging growing conditions, like those in partial shade with moist to wet soil.

▲ Anise hyssop

AGASTACHE FOENICULUM, ZONES 4 TO 8

The anise-scented leaves inspired the common name of this summer bloomer. It thrives in full sun or part shade and in well-draining to dry soil. You'll want to give this 2- to 4-foot plant plenty of room to spread because it readily reseeds.

Why we love it: The lavender flowers also attract butterflies and bees, but deer tend to let it be.

attracts wildlife

▲ Bee balm

MONARDA SPECIES, ZONES 3 TO 9

Rows of red or purple tubular flowers top bee balm's 2- to 4-foot stems throughout summer. Grow this vigorous self-seeder in full sun or partial shade, allowing it plenty of room to expand. The leaves are fragrant when crushed and can be used for tea.

Why we love it: Bee balm's blooms attract a lot of backyard wildlife—hummingbirds, butterflies and bees. Plus, the plants grow successfully near black walnut trees.

▲ Scarlet gilia

IPOMOPSIS RUBRA, ZONES 5 TO 9, BIENNIAL

Watch this plant transform from a mat of feathery foliage the first year to tall stems with finely dissected leaves and tubular red flowers the second year. Also known as standing cypress or Texas plume, gilia thrives in full sun and in well-draining to dry soil.

Why we love it: Scarlet gilia is a biennial that seeds itself, rewarding you with gorgeous flowering plants for many years.

▲ Woodland phlox

PHLOX DIVARICATA, ZONES 3 TO 8

Here's one for the shadows. Grow woodland phlox in partial or full shade and in moist, well-drained soil. Once established, it tolerates drought but does best if you mulch during hot summer months. To reduce the risk of powdery mildew, trim the stems back after the flowers die off.

Why we love it: The rose, lavender or violet-blue flowers are lightly fragrant.

▲ Beardtongue

PENSTEMON SPECIES, ZONES 3 TO 10, VARIES WITH SPECIES

You'll find native penstemon in every state (except Hawaii) and Canadian province. Many varieties bloom in late spring through early summer, while others provide nectar and color from summer until fall. Most tolerate drought. Before growing beardtongue, find one that's native to your area and suited to your growing conditions.

Why we love it: Red beardtongue (*Penstemon barbatus*) is valuable to beneficial insects and attracts large numbers of native bees.

butterfly favorite

▲ Lupine

LUPINUS, ZONES 3 TO 8

There are more than 200 species of lupines, most of which are native to North America. You can find bluebonnets in Texas, annual sky blue and yellow lupines in California, blue pod lupines in the Pacific Northwest and British Columbia, and wild blue lupines throughout much of the country.

Why we love it: While hummingbirds can't get enough of the flowers, birds and small mammals eat the seeds. Karner blue and frosted elfin butterfly larvae feed on the foliage.

▲ Fringed bleeding heart

DICENTRA EXIMIA, ZONES 3 TO 9

You may be surprised to learn this landscape plant is native to the eastern U.S. It blooms later than the larger common bleeding heart, which is native to Asia. The rosy to purplish-red flowers appear in late spring and continue through midsummer on 12- to 18-inch plants. Grow fringed bleeding heart in partial shade and in moist soil for best results.

Why we love it: The fernlike gray-green leaves stay intact and add interest throughout the growing season.

more hummingbird faves

Give them the complete package with vines and shrubs!

- Honeysuckle vine
- Trumpet vine
- Rhododendron
- Azalea
- Blueberry
- Buttonbush
- New Jersey tea
- California lilac

Hummingbird FAQs

Answers to the most common questions about these tricky-to-attract birds.
By Kenn and Kimberly Kaufman

How do I draw hummingbirds to my yard?

Think red! Colorful feeders visible from a distance and classic, tubular flowers are two ways to increase your chances of attracting these birds. It's especially worthwhile adding nectar flowers to your garden and keeping feeders filled and clean at all times.

What can I do about a hummingbird that drives others away from the feeder?

These birds have an instinct to defend their food sources because a patch of flowers produces only a little nectar each day. Even at a feeder, hummingbirds practice the same defensive behavior. A good strategy to prevent one from dominating the food source is to put up several feeders located some distance apart from each other. If a feeder is out of sight from the others (around a corner, for example), it makes it harder for one bird to control them all. In a situation like that, even a more aggressive hummingbird may give up and just share with others.

Which is better, premade or homemade sugar water? Should I add red dye?

Commercial nectar may be convenient, but you can easily make your own. Mix one part white sugar with four parts water. Bring it to a boil to remove impurities so the nectar will keep longer before it starts to spoil. Don't add honey or any other ingredients. Also, avoid red dye. It doesn't help the birds and it may be bad for them.

How do I keep bees, wasps or ants away from my nectar feeders?

The type of feeder makes a difference. In saucer-style feeders, the sugar water is far enough below the feeding ports that insects can't reach it. Some feeders have bee/wasp guards over the feeding ports that deter these insects while allowing hummingbirds to sip. Bee guards won't help if sugar water splashes on the outside of the feeder,

Bee guards give hummingbirds access but prevent bees from taking ownership of feeding ports.

so keep it clean. If ants are a problem, buy a feeder with an ant moat (a small basin of water that acts as a barrier), or get an add-on ant moat that hangs above the feeder.

When should I take my feeders down in fall?

It depends on where you are. In the South and along the Pacific Coast, you may have hummingbirds all winter. Farther north, hummingbirds will probably be gone by October. Later in fall, however, there may be the odd hummingbird from the West showing up in the East. If you keep your feeders up until November, you might attract some surprising visitors. Don't worry that your feeders might keep the locals from migrating. Their migration instinct is very strong. They will leave when they're ready, and neither flowers nor feeders can tempt them to stay.

Multiple birds eating peacefully is rare in most backyards.

glad you asked!

Kenn and Kimberly Kaufman answer your birding questions while Melinda Myers tackles gardening.

Female ruby-throated hummingbird with coneflower

BACKYARD TIP
Coneflowers do best in zones 3 to 9. They'll thrive in a sunny spot and in well-draining soil.

Q&A

I'd like to create and maintain a hummingbird retreat in my backyard. What perennials should I be planting?

Michael Gorss
CENTERVILLE, MASSACHUSETTS

Melinda: Create a garden area filled with hummingbird favorites in a sheltered location. Include spring, summer and fall bloomers to provide three seasons of nectar for these flying beauties. For early blooming, plant bleeding heart, columbine, coral bells and iris. Good summer bloomers are daylilies, penstemon, garden phlox, perennial hibiscus, bee balm, salvia and cardinal flower. Finish off the season with gayfeather (Liatris) and coneflower. Add a few vines like clematis and native honeysuckle vine for vertical interest and more hummingbird appeal. For more plant picks, visit *birdsandblooms.com/ hummingbirds*.

My hummingbird feeders never have visitors. What is the best type of feeder to buy or build?

Lothar Willertz SANFORD, MICHIGAN

Kenn and Kimberly: The traditional glass bottle that threads into a plastic basin works extremely well. We prefer the 30-ounce bottle because it's more stable and doesn't tip as easily when orioles drink from it. We also like the type with a shallow plastic basin where the lid with feeding ports snaps down over it. Both are easy to clean, and that is important. Before giving up on the feeders, make sure you use the proper recipe of four parts water to one part sugar. If the mixture is too weak, birds won't be interested.

DID YOU KNOW?
If you see a hummingbird in a strange position and a sleeplike state, don't fret! It's normal.

This hummingbird visited my backyard. I believe it is a juvenile Anna's or a ruby-throated, but it's so small. Can you help?

Jim McClellan SAN DIEGO, CALIFORNIA

Kenn and Kimberly: Nice close-up! It's amazing how small these birds can look when you get close. But this is actually an adult male, not a juvenile. The adult male Anna's hummingbird is the only hummer in North America that has red on the throat and on the top of the head. Anna's is the most common hummingbird along the California coast, and it's found there year-round. Ruby-throated hummingbirds, so common in the East, are extremely rare visitors to California, with only a few ever recorded.

I saw a hummingbird hanging upside down from my feeder by one foot. As I neared, it flew away. What happened to it?

Margaret Hocker
METROPOLIS, ILLINOIS

Kenn and Kimberly: Hummingbirds have a bizarre way of conserving energy. Usually at night, during periods of cold and sometimes when they're perched at a feeder, hummingbirds can enter a deep, sleeplike state known as torpor, when all body functions slow dramatically. Metabolism slows by as much as 95 percent, and heart rate and body temperature drop significantly. Torpor allows them to conserve precious energy and survive surprisingly low temperatures. Hummingbirds are tough birds!

After watching hummingbirds at my feeders, I noticed that males put their bills farther into the sugar water than females. Do females have longer bills?

Pat Comack
HAZELWOOD, MISSOURI

Kenn and Kimberly: That's an interesting observation! Female ruby-throated hummingbirds do have a slightly longer bill, on average, than males. The difference is so minor—less than one-tenth of an inch—that most people would never notice. The females also average slightly larger bills overall.

BACKYARD TIP
Think you've got an Anna's? They're stockier than other West Coast hummingbirds.

We get Anna's hummingbirds here, but we've never seen this bird before. It showed up for a week in April and sat on the feeder for hours at a time, even at night in the dark. What kind is it?

Pam Brown KENMORE, WASHINGTON

Kenn and Kimberly: Identifying a female hummingbird from a single photo can be very challenging, but we think this is probably just an odd Anna's hummingbird. Color pattern and wing structure rule out every species except Anna's and Costa's hummingbirds, and Costa's is a bird of the desert Southwest that would be a very rare visitor in Washington. Unfortunately, this bird may have been ill, which would explain why it looked unfamiliar to you and why it would just sit on the feeder for long periods.

Female broad-tailed hummingbird

Hummingbirds refuse to eat the sugar water I make with organic sugar. Can you explain the difference between organic and white?

Christine Davis
LUDLOW, MASSACHUSETTS

Kenn and Kimberly:
Pure white table sugar is the safest option for mixing nectar for hummingbirds. Many consider organic sugar, which doesn't tend to be fully refined to pure sucrose, unsafe for feeding hummingbirds.

Female ruby-throated hummingbird

Ruby-throated at lantana

Blooms for Hummingbirds

Follow our field editors' advice and get these favorites in the ground.

1

Autumn sage and trumpet vine are black-chinned hummingbird magnets! The hummingbirds also enjoy hosta and native and noninvasive honeysuckle, but sage is by far their favorite!
Kathy Eppers
ALEDO, TEXAS

2

Hummingbirds find my yard during the end of summer migration, from early August to mid-September. Bee balm attracts them best. The birds always stop by and even go to bee balms when the flowers are just about spent. One summer, calliope, rufous and ruby-throat all showed up here!
Ken Orich
LETHBRIDGE, ALBERTA

3

Hummingbirds swarm to canna, butterfly bush and hosta in my yard, flitting around from sunrise to sunset. On rare occasions, I've even had black-chinned and buff-bellied stop by to visit.
Joan Heid
CHESTER, SOUTH CAROLINA

4

We get Anna's hummingbirds visiting year-round. They hang around fuchsia, hibiscus and occasionally snapdragons and princess flowers. But mostly, they love my sugar-water feeder.
Katherine Reseburg
SAUSALITO, CALIFORNIA

5

To get the most nectar in spring and fall, I plant tons of salvia. I try to plant taller varieties—Black and Blue, Hot Lips, Maraschino and Amistad. My other go-to plants are crocosmia, red-hot poker and penstemon.
Connie Etter
MARTINSVILLE, INDIANA

Hand-Feed Hummingbirds

Experience the thrill of tiny bird feet perched on your finger. **By Sally Roth**

There are plenty of videos online of lucky people hand-feeding hummingbirds. It's incredible to watch, but if you've always yearned for the excitement of seeing delicate hummingbirds up close, here's how you can do it, too.

Be part of the scene.
The easiest way to get close to the action is to be in the middle of it. Study the traffic at your hummingbird feeder and find out when it's busiest (usually after dawn and before dusk). If you have multiple nectar feeders, remove all but one. Then, put a bench or lawn chair beside the feeder and sit as still as possible. Do this often enough and eventually your presence will be accepted and ignored.

Use your hand as a perch.
Patience is required here, but this is really where things can get exciting. Hold the feeder in your lap and extend a finger as a perch. Stay as motionless as you can, and eventually, you might feel a hummingbird settle on your outstretched finger. Wait until no hummingbirds are present before you remove your hand.

Buy or make a hand feeder.
Feeder designers know how beloved hummingbirds are, and that is why they created feeders that fit into your hand. Inexpensive miniature hand feeders can be purchased online or at local bird supply stores, and they work like a charm. You also can make one from a vial, a narrow glass jar or other small container. Wrap a red ribbon around the top of a homemade feeder, then attach a plastic feeder "flower" to the top of your vial or bottle. Hummingbirds use those clues to know where to insert their bills.

Try the bait-and-switch technique.
It's easy enough to hold your hand feeder beside the usual nectar feeder. To speed things up, especially in ruby-throated hummingbird regions, remove the usual feeder when no hummingbirds are present, and hold out your hand feeder in its place. Prop your arm on a deck railing or the back of a chair so you can wait comfortably. And if your feet get itchy, stroll around your yard with the hand feeder, and when you see a hummingbird at a flower, hold out the feeder!

CLOSE ENCOUNTERS
A reader shares her story.

Last summer, I started spending 15 minutes each day standing as motionless as possible next to my hummingbird feeder. My daily visitors quickly got used to my presence. One hummingbird was bold enough to buzz around my head so close I could feel the wind from its wings against my hair.

My brother-in-law gave me a handheld feeder for my birthday, and within five minutes a hummingbird was eating out of my hand! The hummingbird moved back and forth between the feeders, seemingly in no hurry to leave. This is one birding experience that will stay with me for many years to come.

Lorraine Hoffman
GREENSBURG, PENNSYLVANIA

TROUBLESHOOTING TIPS
Boost your chances of hummingbird hand-feeding success.

- Use a 1:3 ratio (1 part sugar to 3 parts water) to make your handheld feeder extra appealing from the first taste. Once the birds are accustomed to it, go back to the typical 1:4.
- Fill the hand feeder to the brim so that hummingbirds get a payoff as soon as they dip in their beaks.
- Hand-feed ruby-throated hummingbirds at the same time every day and when their numbers are at their highest; spring and fall migration is your best opportunity.

hummer happenings

Your bird tales celebrate all things hummingbird.

One rainy Saturday morning, my husband and I noticed a ruby-throated hummingbird relishing the rain. These birds are usually in motion, so it was a peaceful sight to see this hummingbird perched contentedly, neck stretched with its head to the sky, truly enjoying the moment. I snapped this photo through our kitchen window. I love the idea that this little bird was stopping to enjoy the cool rain!

Mary Meyer
EYOTA, MINNESOTA

DID YOU KNOW
In downpours, hummingbirds will shake their heads and bodies to dry off, similar to the way dogs do.

I took this photo in a Utah park. There were several feeders and more than 20 hummingbirds zipping around. These birds tend to be elusive, flying away before you can get a good look at them. Having so many in one spot allowed for this interesting shot with another bird out of focus in the background. These birds are like magic, and each time I look at the photographs I've taken of them, I remember hearing the unique sound of their wings and bodies cutting through the air.

Helene Bushnell LOWELL, MASSACHUSETTS

Last spring,
I set up feeders in the hopes of finally attaining my dream of having a hummingbird-friendly backyard. Within a few days, I had my first visitors, but my next challenge was to photograph them. I spent hours patiently waiting to get the perfect shot. The day I took this photo, the sun was filtering through the trees in my neighbor's backyard, creating a stunning backdrop. A lone male calliope took his position at the feeder, and with a few quick clicks of my camera, he was gone. But I got my shot!

Tiffany Hansen
SPOKANE, WASHINGTON

This male Costa's hummingbird
is actually guarding "his" feeder. Any time another Costa's, black-chinned or Anna's would land on the feeder, he would dash out from his hiding place in this pomegranate bush, scare away his competition and return to the exact same branch every time. His stubbornness made it easy for me to set up my camera, aim and get several good pictures.

Carla Ritter IVINS, UTAH

amazing hummingbirds 97

The sun was peeking over the tree line, and I stood with a cup of coffee watching God's creation unfold. The bloom on the orchid cactus my sister gave me was opening, so I wanted a picture of it to send to her. Right then, a hummingbird flitted over to check out the flower. With the sun shining perfectly on the bloom, I captured this wonderful moment.

Patrick Henderson MATTHEWS, NORTH CAROLINA

My wife decided she wanted to have hummingbirds in our backyard, so she went to a local bird store and bought this feeder. I thought there was no way it was going to work, but within a week, there was a hummingbird! Photographing these fast little creatures was a challenge. In the beginning, my shots were really bad, but I'd try a different technique each time, and ended up getting this shot. Practice really does make perfect.

Robert Shepler
SYLVANIA, OHIO

DID YOU KNOW?
Black-eyed Susans attract many kinds of wildlife, including birds, butterflies, slugs, snails and aphids.

There was a lot of congestion at the feeders one summer evening, but this female ruby-throated hummingbird waited until all the drama at the "water cooler" was over before taking her turn. I've seen hummingbirds in trees and on feeder perches and posts, but this was the first time I'd witnessed one using a black-eyed Susan as a resting place.

Jon Montgomery
DU QUOIN, ILLINOIS

This male calliope was the first arrival of the year, stopping by our backyard in mid-April. During the colder spring weather, he would perch on this stick close to the feeder. The blurry pink background is thanks to our crabapple tree, which was in full bloom across the yard.

Bill Bolster MEDICAL LAKE, WASHINGTON

Ruby-throated hummingbird
Photo by Rolf Nussbaumer

Ruby-throated hummingbird
Photo by MBolina/iStock

Rufous/Allen's hummingbird
Finalist in our
Backyard Photo Contest
Photo by Nancy Albert

Broad-tailed hummingbird
Photo by Sharon Draker

Leucistic hummingbird
Finalist in our
Backyard Photo Contest
Photo by Sharon Draker

CHAPTER 3

DIY Projects

Dress up a backyard, whether big or small, with the fun do-it-yourself garden ideas found here. Grow savory herbs indoors in tin cans, hang a beautifully crafted birdhouse and create clever handmade feeders within moments.

HEIDI HESS

Landscaping Tips for Mini Gardens

- Mass plantings are more effective than several individual plants.
- Put larger plants in the back of the container and lower plants in the front.
- Arrange the garden path or stream so it "disappears" beyond the foliage to create a sense of depth.
- Add a focal point, like the birdhouse at the end of the path shown here.
- Use a single blossom or leaf bundle as an accent.

Enchanting Mini Garden

Transform an old birdbath into a tiny landscape.

By Alison Auth

STEP 1. Before planting, place a birdbath or other container, such as a terra-cotta pot or wooden box, where it will stay permanently. (It will be too heavy to move later.)

STEP 2. Play around with the landscape design with the plants still in their pots to make things easier on you and the plants.

STEP 3. Fill the planter about two-thirds full with soil.

STEP 4. Remove plants from their pots one at a time, knock off soil, and loosen and spread out roots. If roots are matted, spray with a hose to detangle them, then gently pull them apart as necessary so they splay out in the soil.

STEP 5. Position the plants in the soil by spreading the roots of each as widely as you can, leaving room for neighboring plants. This step is especially important if you are using a birdbath or similarly shallow planter.

STEP 6. Once you're satisfied with the arrangement, add as much soil as possible to cover the roots, but not so much that watering will wash it away.

STEP 7. Gently water all plants with a watering can or by holding your thumb over a hose nozzle to make a fine spray.

STEP 8. Add features. Try using everyday items in a new way: Gravel can be a tiny stone path; tumbled glass transforms into a shimmering pond. Fairy garden decorations, sold online or at hobby stores, range from minuscule arbors and bridges to tiny houses and animal figurines. Just one will lend scale to your miniature garden.

Miniature Plant Picks
Not sure where to start? Try these on for size.

SUCCULENTS
Use them for accent plants or "shrubs."

Stonecrop sedum
Limelight sedum
Blue Spruce sedum
Silver Onion echeveria
Hens-and-chicks

GROUND COVERS
Create a mat of green in the miniature garden, and a "waterfall" over the planter.

Golden club moss (*Selaginella kraussiana* 'Aurea')
Scotch moss (*Sagina subulata* 'Aurea')
Blue Star creeper
Pink cranesbill (*Erodium* x *variabile* 'Bishop's Form')

CONIFERS
Provide woodland "shade" and a layer of realism.

Jervis dwarf Canadian hemlock
Dwarf Pagoda Japanese holly
Mont Bruno boxwood
Fernspray false cypress
Lime Glow juniper

Easy-to-Make Feeders

These four feeders are inexpensive, simple to create and great projects for kids on rainy days. Grab a few supplies and get crafting!

supplies

- Bucket
- Water
- Newspaper (about 10 pages, cut in strips)
- Duct tape
- Window screen
- Drill with drill bits
- Fishing line
- Beads
- Peanut butter
- Birdseed
- Wire hanger

1 Paper Heart Feeder

STEP 1. Fill a bucket half full with water and add newspaper strips. Allow the paper to soak for about 15 minutes. Then squish and roll the paper in your hands to extract the water. Repeat this process a few times until the paper is in very small pieces.

STEP 2. Use duct tape to attach a window screen to the top of the bucket.

STEP 3. Rinse the pieces of paper a few more times by pouring them over the screen to remove most of the water. Squish and roll the paper again; put in a clean bucket of water. Repeat until most of the ink is washed away.

STEP 4. Pour the paper over your screen one last time. Allow it to sit for a while so most of the water is removed. You want it wet, but not so wet it won't mold into your shape. Begin shaping your paper into a softball-sized heart (or a different shape of your choice). The base of your paper feeder should be about an inch thick. Allow it to dry.

STEP 5. Drill a hole through the top of each side of the heart. Thread a piece of fishing line through one hole, tie and add beads. Thread the line through the other hole and tie.

STEP 6. Spread peanut butter on each side of the paper heart feeder and dip into birdseed. Then just hang it up!

more decorating ideas

Create more shapes, like moons and stars. String cranberries or popcorn instead of beads to the fishing line. Use your imagination and make this feeder your own!

4 Tin Can Flower Feeder

STEP 1. On the side of each tin can, use a ruler to measure about 1/4 in. from each end in a straight line. Then mark a dot at each of these points with a permanent marker. Use a drill or metal punch to make holes about 1/4 in. wide where the marked dots are. These two holes are where you will insert the twine for making a hanger later on.

STEP 2. In a well-ventilated area, spray-paint the outside of your tin cans in various colors. Apply as many coats as needed for full coverage and let dry 24-48 hours.

STEP 3. Center the open end of each can on a foam flower. Trace around the circle opening with a pencil. Working freehand or with a compass, draw another circle, about 1/2 in. smaller, centered in the first circle. Then use a ruler to draw several crisscrossing straight lines inside the original traced circle (the way a pizza is cut). Cut out the small inner circle. Then cut along each crisscrossing line, stopping at the traced outline of the original circle. This will make several tabs around the inner perimeter.

STEP 4. Lay the foam flower face down on a flat surface. Apply a ring of hot glue around the perimeter of the traced circle. Then place the open end of the can aligned on top of the hot glue ring. Hold the can firmly in place until the glue dries. Hot glue each of the cut tabs down on the interior of the can rim to further secure the foam flower in place.

STEP 5. For the hangers, first cut a piece of twine 12-18 in. long for each of your cans. Thread one end through the back hole, inside the can and back up through the front hole. With even lengths of twine, place several large beads on each loose end. Knot the top of the twine to secure the hanger with beads in place. Repeat for each tin can feeder. Fill can with birdseed and hang.

2 Decorative Suet Ball Feeder

STEP 1. Prepare your favorite suet recipe. Then fill an orange half with it.

STEP 2. Insert sticks for perches.

STEP 3. Hang with natural twine.

3 Milk Carton Feeder

STEP 1. Poke a twig through the lower center of a small milk carton to serve as a perch.

STEP 2. Liberally spread peanut butter over the milk carton. Sprinkle with birdseed all around it.

STEP 3. Add raisins, if desired, and make a hole to thread a ribbon through the top of the milk carton.

STEP 4. Slip it onto a tree branch and wait for the birds to flock to their new feeder.

supplies

- Clean, opened tin cans with labels removed
- Drill with drill bits or metal punch
- Spray paint in choice of colors
- Precut 6-in.-wide foam flowers (available at most craft stores)
- Hot glue gun and glue sticks
- Thick twine
- Large wooden or plastic beads

Burning Beauty

Build your own birdhouse from scratch and add a personal touch with a burned-in pattern. **By Alison Auth**

supplies

- One 5-ft. 1-by-6 No. 2 common pine board
- Handsaw or compound miter saw
- Power drill and bits
- 1¼- to 1⅝-in. spade bit or hole saw
- Eight 1⅝-in. galvanized deck screws
- Six 2-in. galvanized finishing nails
- Fine-grit sandpaper
- Carbon or tracing paper (optional)
- Wood-burning kit or pen
- Sponge or honing paper

BIRDHOUSE

STEP 1. Measure and cut the pine board into 5 pieces:

    A. 10-in. piece for front

    B. 10-in. piece for roof

    C. 7¾-in. piece for back

    D. 18-in. piece for sides

    E. 4-in. piece for floor

Save the remaining scrap board for wood-burning practice.

STEP 2. For sides, on D, measure and mark 8 in. along the top and 10 in. along the bottom. Draw a line connecting the points. Cut along this diagonal to yield 2 pieces, each with an 8-in. and a 10-in. side.

STEP 3. With spade bit or hole saw, on A (front), drill entrance hole 2-2½ in. from a short side.

STEP 4. On front side of A, drill through each corner with a narrow bit, then attach A to 10-in. sides of D with four 1⅝-in. deck screws.

STEP 5. Attach C (back) to center of the 8-in. sides of D with two 2-in. finishing nails. Predrill holes in C using a slightly smaller bit.

STEP 6. Cut about ½ in. off each corner of E (floor) for drainage gaps when house is complete.

STEP 7. Set the floor ¼ in. up from the bottom of the house, then attach it with four 2-in. finishing nails at the sides and back. (Do not nail the floor at the front, or you won't be able to unscrew the birdhouse front for cleaning.)

STEP 8. Attach B (roof) to top at sides with four 1⅝-in. deck screws. Predrill holes in B with a narrow bit.

BURNING

STEP 9. Sand the exterior of the birdhouse smooth, including the entrance hole, with fine-grit sandpaper.

STEP 10. Use carbon paper to trace a design onto the wood, or draw it freehand.

STEP 11. With burner pen at desired temperature, follow the pattern, being careful not to put too much pressure on the pen tip. When the pattern is finished, hang the birdhouse in your favorite backyard spot.

WOOD-BURNING TIPS

- Before you start burning the pattern onto the birdhouse, practice on a scrap of pine to determine the best heat setting and to get comfortable with the process.
- Because of the heat, carbon will build up on the metal pen tips. Keep a damp sponge or honing paper near the work space to wipe off the tip.
- For the cleanest lines, go slowly and maintain consistent pressure. You can change the look of the burn by altering the pressure and the length of time the tip is on the wood.

effortless
winter containers

Greet guests with simple yet spectacular cold-weather containers. **By Crystal Rennicke**

Winter is gloomy for gardeners. Gray skies are a bleak backdrop for a barren yard, but you can lift your spirits and add welcome color by planting winter containers. You may only need to walk around your yard or nearby woods to find supplies, and the results will wow holiday visitors.

USE NATURE
Take a walk through your backyard and look for accessories for winter containers. Pinecones, holly and even twigs make great accents.

Experiment with trees and shrubs; find dwarf varieties of your favorites and prune as necessary to keep them small and manageable.

Hunt and Gather

Before you head to the garden center, step outside your back door and forage for materials right at your fingertips. Look for things with unique texture, form and color. Here are some ideas for happy hunting:

Perennials: A general rule of thumb is to use perennials, trees and shrubs that are hardy to two zones colder than your own when planting in containers. Because the roots are elevated and aren't insulated by a blanket of soil, they'll need extra protection. However, there are a few diehards for some of the coldest climates like dwarf white pine, dwarf Alberta spruce, some boxwood, juniper and ornamental grasses.

Branches: Look for branches with height, texture and color. Cut a few stems off your red or yellow twig dogwood. Or plant the entire dogwood in your container as a year-round standout in your arrangement. If you have them, the quirky-looking branches of birch, curly willow, Harry Lauder's walking stick or paperbark maple are great options. Snip off a few boughs from your Christmas tree or other evergreen.

Dried material: At the end of the growing season, look for late-season flowers like allium, astilbe or hydrangea and dry them in a warm place or right in the garden. Find fluffy seed heads of ornamental grasses to save for your containers. Stop deadheading your roses in late summer to spur them on to produce colorful rose hips for your arrangements.

Berries: Cut off a few branches from your winterberry shrub with its gorgeous clusters of bright red berries. Forage for firethorn, sumac or holly berries as well.

Other accents: Look for pinecones or pine needles outdoors. Inside your home, search for a few festive accents such as glass icicles, artificial berries, solar lights, and birdseed or plastic tree ornaments.

Containers for Cold

Think of your container as an investment and buy the best quality you can afford. Find frostproof, durable ones that you can use

Switchgrass

Ice Dance carex

Red twig dogwood

Boxwood

Angelina sedum

HARDY PLANTS

(choose 1-2)

Dwarf Alberta spruce, *Picea glauca* 'Conica', Zones 2 to 8

Ornamental grasses (try switchgrass, *Panicum virgatum*, Zones 4 to 9, or sedge, *Carex* 'Ice Dance', Zones 5 to 9)

Red twig dogwood, *Cornus sericea*, Zones 2 to 8

Flaviramea yellow twig dogwood, *Cornus sericea* 'Flaviramea', Zones 2 to 8

Golden Sword yucca, *Yucca filamentosa* 'Golden Sword', Zones 4 to 11

Green Gem boxwood, *Buxux sempervirens* 'Green Gem', Zones 4 to 9

Angelina sedum, *Sedum rupestre* 'Angelina', Zones 3 to 9

Snow Angel heuchera *Heuchera sanguinea* 'Snow Angel', Zones 3 to 8

Little King dwarf river birch, *Betula nigra* 'Little King', Zones 3 to 7

FRESH-CUT BOUGHS OR BERRIES

(choose 2-4)

Arborvitae

Winterberry

False cypress

Orange winterberry

Firethorn

Red twig dogwood

Yellow twig dogwood

Birch

Curly willow

Paperbark maple

Harry Lauder's walking stick

Evergreens (spruce, white pine, juniper)

ACCENTS

Pinecones

Solar string lights

Glass or plastic icicles

Plastic ornaments

Artificial berries

Spray paint

Ribbon

---

year-round. Urns are perfect for winter container combinations.

Cement, concrete, iron or stone are the most durable, but are also a tad expensive (and heavy!). If you're on a budget, use high-quality resin, wood or fiberglass containers. Avoid using ceramic containers or terra-cotta pots. They hold moisture and can chip or crack with repeated freezing and thawing.

Remember, the bigger the container, the more insulation for those precious plant roots. Make sure the pot has adequate drainage and fill it to nearly full with a well-draining potting mix. If it's a container you use year-round, you can simply leave the soil inside.

Don't be afraid to use something you already own! We've seen winter containers made of wrought-iron baskets or balls, chicken wire, lanterns and even an old pair of ice skates!

Simple Assembly

Once you have your materials and container, get started assembling. Use a mix of perennials, freshly cut boughs, berries, dried materials and accents.

Think of perennials and branches as the backbone for your winter container. They add structure to the planting, and interest year-round. Experiment with trees and shrubs; Find dwarf varieties of your favorites and prune as necessary to keep them small and manageable.

If you're starting with new perennials, make sure they have adequate time to acclimate to the container before frost. Water them thoroughly until you have a hard freeze—then stop watering.

With your perennials in place, add other branches, if necessary. Stick dogwood, willow or other tall branches inside to make the container appear grand and full. Fill it in with freshly cut evergreen boughs. Continue with berried branches and other dried materials. Keep a close eye on uniformity throughout and from all angles.

To keep branches and boughs from drying out in the winter winds, apply an antidesiccant like Wilt-Pruf. Mist berries with a commercially available wax spray to lock in moisture and

keep them on branches through the bitter cold. Or look for artificial berries sold specifically for outdoor use. They won't expand and crack like other artificial berries.

Embellish with Ease

Once you have a combination that looks full, accent it with other items. Intersperse your container with clusters of pinecones. Spray-paint your branches with glitter or paint. Include a string of tiny solar lights for a bit of magic after dark. Add a ribbon, bow or plastic ornaments for a finishing touch. If you're using ribbon, use a waterproof, color-safe one that is labeled for outdoor use.

If you've planted a shrub in a container that doesn't have winter interest, it's easy to dress it up. Add a birdseed wreath (just roll a craft wreath in peanut butter and birdseed) and place it around the lip of the pot, or add birdseed ornaments and lights for a look the birds will love, too!

Get creative with what winter has to offer. You'll be surprised how fast your landscape can go from drab to fab with just a couple of winter containers.

Tin Can Herb Set

Welcome spring with a tabletop herb garden.
By Pam Stasney

supplies

- 3 recycled soup cans
- Drill
- 3 herb plants
- Potting soil
- Burlap ribbon, extra-wide
- Glue gun
- Craft glue
- Burlap lace ribbons, various widths
- 3 flat wood ovals
- Jute twine
- Fine-point paint pen, white
- 3 oval stickers, black
- Card stock scraps
- 3 wood skewers
- Metal pie plate
- Small decorative rocks

MAKE IT YOUR OWN
If burlap and lace aren't your style, use any fabric and ribbon combo you like. Or spray-paint the outside of the cans for a sleek look.

STEP 1. Remove labels from cans. Wash cans with soap and water, removing any label residue.

STEP 2. Drill a small hole through the bottom of each can for drainage. Repot each plant in a can, adding potting soil as needed.

STEP 3. Wrap a piece of extra-wide ribbon around each can; overlap ends. Fold overlapping edge under to create a hem; hot-glue hem.

STEP 4. Wrap a piece of lace ribbon around the wide ribbon on each can, varying the lace widths among the cans, and glue as in Step 3, positioning the overlapped ends over the previous ends.

STEP 5. Trace wood oval on wide burlap ribbon and cut out 3 burlap ovals. Using craft glue, adhere a burlap oval to each wood oval, matching edges. Trim edges to neaten, if needed.

STEP 6. Hot-glue a border of twine around the burlap oval edges for a finished look.

STEP 7. For each plant marker, use paint pen to write an herb name on a sticker. Attach sticker to a card stock scrap, and trim card edge even with sticker. Hot-glue sticker assembly to the center of a burlap oval.

STEP 8. Hot-glue the blunt end of a skewer to the back of each assembled herb marker. Let dry completely.

STEP 9. Place plants in pie plate. Add markers. Arrange rocks around cans in pie plate as desired.

Metal Yard Art

Use your imagination to create a bird sculpture out of an old light fixture.
By Alison Auth

supplies

- Assorted disassembled lamp pieces
- Flower stake
- 2 tin cans
- Snips
- Hole punch
- Needle-nose pliers

STEP 1. Play around with the disassembled lamp pieces by arranging them in different ways to see what your final bird might look like. Choose a favorite combination.

STEP 2. A lamp rod is what holds everything together. Drill a hole in a finial (the fancy topper) if it doesn't already have one, and slide it and a few more pieces onto the rod to create the bird's head. (Don't forget to leave some extra lamp rod for the rest of the body.) Then secure a flower stake to the rod.

STEP 3. Now it's time for the wings. Cut one long wing-shaped piece from a tin can, punch a hole in the center

PRO TIP
Alison used a combination of lamp candle cups, couplings, washers and tomato paste cans to make the cute hummingbird shown here.

and slide it onto the rod. We bent the wings on our hummingbird to make it look as if it's flying. Secure the wings in place and slide on a couple of pieces to round out the body.

STEP 4. Cut two tail feathers from a tin can and slide them onto the lamp rod. Use a washer with a nut to tighten the feathers against the body.

STEP 5. Prevent rust by spraying your bird creation with clear lacquer or acrylic sealer. Stake the bird in a garden or in a planter.

Inspiring Ideas
Animal sculptures can be made from all sorts of household items.

BROKEN YARD TOOLS
Shovels, stiff or flexible rakes, wooden handles and smaller hand tools are great for tails, heads, bodies, wings and feet for larger yard sculptures.

PLUMBING PARTS
Supply hoses, valves, bathtub and sink handles, hose bibs, threaded pipes and a vast array of brass fittings are easy to assemble into an animal.

FURNACE AND GAS FITTINGS
Copper furnace supply lines or black metal gas pipes and fittings can be ideal animal armatures.

ELECTRICAL SUPPLIES
Metal conduit and fittings, copper wire, fuses, plugs, worn-out circuit breakers, lamp parts and even outlet covers can be repurposed.

HARDWARE AND TIN CANS
Magnets, nuts, bolts and similar hardware attached to tin cans create whimsical creatures. Door hinges, big bolts, doorknobs, springs and a host of other everyday items can serve as sources for animal inspiration.

attracting Birds

Grow your own birdseed with advice from experts, and find out what plants birds can't resist. Change up the menu to keep birds visiting your yard year-round. Discover what attracts tanagers, bluebirds and finches.

STEVE AND DAVE MASLOWSKI

grow your own seed

Bring your landscape to life

An American goldfinch plucks a seed from a sunflower head.

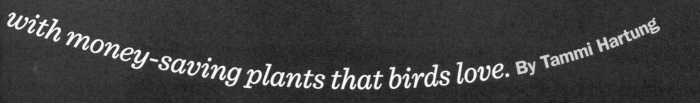

with money-saving plants that birds love. **By Tammi Hartung**

CHANCES ARE birds eagerly accept your open invitation to dine at your feeders. Make birds more permanent guests by adding plants they love to eat.

In fact, the more bird-friendly plants you grow, the less time you spend filling feeders and buying seed. Plant a combination of seed-producing annuals and perennials to supply food year-round while saving time and money. Not all your favorite guests have the same palate, so diversity is key.

Host indigo buntings and other birds when you grow coneflowers.

most wanted birds

Look for these seedeaters flitting from plant to plant.

Chickadees
Dark-eyed juncos
Goldfinches
Grosbeaks
House finches
Nuthatches
Northern cardinals
Pine siskins
Purple finches

Yarrow varieties attract seedeaters like pine siskins.

SERVE UP THE PERFECT PLANTS

Lure more small songbirds to your garden with a selection of early-flowering perennials. Lavender, with its blue and purple flower stalks, bursts onto the garden scene in early summer. The purple spikes of anise hyssop bloom in early summer and continue into August, but some are very aggressive, so choose carefully. Yarrows, available in white and shades of yellow and pink, shine off and on throughout summer, too. To add a little color variation, consider columbines. Most columbines grow in full sun to part shade, but native varieties also work well in shady garden beds. All these perennials yield seed heads that are fantastic food sources for chickadees and juncos, especially after flowers have faded. American goldfinches and other types of finches, along with pine siskins and indigo buntings, eat up the small seeds as well.

Summer's brightest blooms provide a buffet of food options for feathered friends. Purple coneflowers have beautiful purplish-pink petals and burnt orange centers. After petals fade, the center cones have tasty seeds that nuthatches and pine siskins devour. Black-eyed Susans and sunflowers come alive in midsummer with cheerful yellow flowers for a colorful garden show well into early fall. Several seedeaters, including eastern and California towhees, forage these noninvasive plants.

The purple and pink blooms of buddleia bushes (choose noninvasive types) add color all summer and into fall. As flowers fade and seeds form, sparrows and finches feed on them. Joe Pye weed's mauve flowers complement showy fans of bright yellow goldenrod in late summer. Both dazzle into midautumn and attract indigo and lazuli buntings. And sedum works, too—many small songbirds feast on the dried flowers after the white, pink or yellow clusters fade.

Aloha coneflower

Pink yarrow

Add water to make your yard more appealing to birds.

PLAN A GREAT SPACE

Growing plants for birds is crucial, but it's just one part of the equation. Several other actions create a well-rounded and thriving environment that attracts multiple bird species.

Be cautious about using chemicals. Direct-contact or broadcast applications are harmful if birds eat seeds treated with insecticides or synthetic pesticides. Because chemicals leave residue inside plant parts for up to 18 months, it's best to keep natural spaces free of any pesticides, fungicides and herbicides.

Next, set up a good water source to help birds wash down a meal. Birds need only about an inch of water, but if your birdbath is somewhat deep, add a good-sized rock in the center as a solid perching spot.

When all flowers have flourished for the season, keep your garden intact. The less tidying you do, the better. Leave dried flower heads in place for foraging winter birds. Cut back and clean up last year's stalks in late winter and early spring when you're ready to prep for the new season.

Once you attract seedeaters to your space, you won't want them to leave. Small songbirds provide hours of entertainment and delight as they forage and find food. But more important, the habitat you create gives your favorite fliers a much-needed healthy haven to return to again and again.

Joe Pye weed

the secret's in the sunflowers

Plant several of these varieties to get more birds for your buck.

Autumn Beauty: multiple flowers in yellow, burgundy and gold
Fat Mama: traditional with fat flower heads
Lyng's California Greystripe: large yellow flowers that give way to gray and white striped seeds
Maximilian: multibranched with lots of 3-inch yellow blooms
Mexican (Tithonia): loads of orange flowers that attract pollinators

Moulin Rouge: deep burgundy petals with a rich black center
Ring of Fire: yellow petals with a dark red ring around the center
Strawberry Blonde: lemony tips and rose-pink petals with a dark center
Taiyo: a Japanese heirloom with large chocolate brown centers and short yellow petals
Teddy Bear: double yellow flowers on dwarf plants

Sunflowers lure songbirds, like this song sparrow, to your backyard.

Plants for Birds
Field editors share their favorite bird-friendly plant picks.

1
A favorite is, believe it or not, catnip! It brings in hummingbirds and other birds that eat bugs and nectar, along with seedeaters and all kinds of insects. I was very surprised to see that. We have a catnip plant that came up under our bird feeders, and I've taken some nice photos of the goldfinches enjoying its bounty.
Suzanne Cassidy
HUGHESVILLE, MARYLAND

2
We have liatris throughout our perennial gardens. Ruby-throated hummingbirds visit it constantly when it's in bloom. When the liatris goes to seed, we see goldfinches, purple finches, song sparrows, chipping sparrows, white-crowned sparrows, chickadees, cardinals, titmice and even migrating warblers.
Keith Golden
LAKE CARROLL, ILLINOIS

3
Our Sargent crabapple attracts nesting robins. It also attracts cedar waxwings in fall and in winter. We usually have robins that will stay, even in winter, until the waxwings come and strip the tree of its fruit.
Ken Wellnitz
DAVENPORT, IOWA

4
Our elderberry attracts warblers, waxwings, orioles, hummingbirds and sparrows galore (Savannah, song, chipping and, unfortunately, house). It's a great little bush.
Jen St. Louis
ELMIRA, ONTARIO

5
My butterfly bushes attract cardinals, nuthatches, chickadees and many other birds. The birds hide in the bush and watch butterflies, bees and hummingbirds drink nectar from the blossoms.
Joan Heid
CHESTER, SOUTH CAROLINA

365 Feeding Birds Days a Year

Switch up what you're serving to attract more birds to your backyard. **By Ken Keffer**

Don't forget about bird-friendly plants. Mountain ash trees attract a ton of birds, including this female pine grosbeak.

House finches and a cardinal eating seed.

I tend to notice the changing of the seasons

by bird activity, not weather. When I see the first migrating sparrows return to my hedgerow, I know spring is on the way. And when juvenile birds are fluttering their wings and begging for food, it's summer. These sights can be huge hints that it's time to make some changes to your feeding routine. Follow this guide, and you'll have a robust bird presence in your yard year-round.

Attract Steller's (shown here) and blue jays with peanut feeders.

Winter

Even in the harshest of winters, birds can find plenty of natural food sources. But they will regularly hit up backyard feeding stations for a steady food supply.

Foods that are higher in fat can give birds an extra boost. Try offering up peanuts, either in the shell or without. In most feeders you can mix unshelled peanuts with sunflower seeds. Or you can try feeding peanuts separately. While the chipmunks are curled up for a long winter's nap, you can bet the squirrels will be interested in peanuts all winter long. (And so will the jays, chickadees and woodpeckers.)

Suet can be offered year-round, but in wintertime it's especially popular with woodpeckers, nuthatches, titmice

Evening and pine grosbeaks and downy woodpeckers frequent feeders, especially during cold months in the northern U.S.

and chickadees. Even odd visitors, like pine warblers, may stop in to sample suet.

Spring

With the arrival of spring comes the return of exciting migrating species. As these spring migrants start to arrive, you should enforce the spring-cleaning rule. Be honest—you didn't keep your feeders exceptionally clean over the long winter, did you? Cleaning your feeding stations regularly will help cut down on disease transmission and deter unwelcome visitors like raccoons.

As temperatures heat up in most of the country, it's also the best time to hang nectar feeders for orioles and hummingbirds. These backyard favorites reach the Gulf Coast by late February or early March and have made it northward by Mother's Day. You'll have the best success attracting orioles if you offer grape jelly or oranges in addition to nectar. Orioles aren't the only ones that have a sweet tooth…er, beak. Gray catbirds, northern mockingbirds and American robins also make special appearances at feeders in the spring.

Lastly, don't shy away from mealworms in the spring. They tend to be bluebird magnets, so if they aren't on your menu, give them a try. If you're not ready for live mealworms yet, buy dried ones. You might be surprised to see woodpeckers and chickadees stopping for mealworms, too!

attracting birds   **127**

Attract golden-fronted woodpeckers by putting out orange halves, grapes or mangoes.

Yellow-rumped warblers visit feeders for seeds and suet, but they prefer berries in fall, like this bayberry.

Summer

Nesting birds and fledglings steal the spotlight in summer. The antics of young birds crash landing in the backyard will make anyone smile. It's easy to lure nesting birds to your yard by providing nesting material. Plenty of species use natural materials to line their nests.

It's important to be selective about what you offer, though. Most synthetic materials (and some natural ones, like cotton) can actually do more harm than good, especially when they're wet. Although commercial nesting-material blends are available, you can create a buffet of natural materials for the birds by gathering up twigs, grasses or other plant material from your own backyard. Throw some of your pet's hair in there, too. Some folks just toss materials around the backyard, while others use suet cages to hold the nesting material in place.

Another summer attraction is water. A birdbath is a nice touch, but moving water is even more irresistible to birds. Try adding a spinner, bubbler or fountain to your birdbath to see if it attracts any new guests. Water misters are also an option. Hummingbirds have been known to dart in and out of the fine spray, preferring that to traditional birdbaths.

When it comes to serving food in summer, don't rule out suet. No-melt suet cakes are out there, and they typically have more cornmeal in them, so they tend to be less of an oozy mess for those in warmer climates. Nuthatches and woodpeckers will enjoy them even in summer.

Fall

Autumn is a season of movement for many birds. Migrants are headed toward their wintering grounds, but even local birds shift around in their ranges as they settle in for winter. It's also harvest season in your garden, so let the birds do a little harvesting of their own. Leave your sunflowers and coneflowers alone and let the birds eat seeds straight from the source. Berry producers like dogwood, currant or bayberry can also attract fall birds. A flock of cedar waxwings might even devour all of the berries on your trees and shrubs in one quick fall visit.

As summer turns to autumn, many people take their hummingbird feeders down. Keep them up for a bit longer, and you might be rewarded with a rare treat. Hummingbirds sometimes show up in unexpected places during fall migration. Rufous hummingbirds, a Western species, are increasingly seen in the Midwest and East at this time. Other Western and Southwestern species, such as black-chinned, Anna's, Costa's and broad-billed, have been reported far to the North and East in the fall. A good rule of thumb is to keep your feeder up for at least two weeks after you've last seen a hummingbird.

Feeding backyard birds can bring year-round enjoyment to your life. It'll only take a short time for you to be more in tune with the changes happening around you. These seasonal patterns will become familiar, and you'll find yourself no longer marking the seasons by the weather but instead by the birds.

Dried sunflower heads attract birds like white-breasted nuthatches.

DOs and DON'Ts for DIY Seed Mix

Save money and make your own birdseed blend.

eat millet, it might be a good idea to skip it when customizing your own birdseed.

DO create fun shapes.

Combine your homemade seed mix with unflavored gelatin and water, spread it on a cookie sheet and let it chill. Then, form it into shapes like wreaths, stars, hearts, or use whatever cookie cutters you've got on hand.

DO experiment.

Watch the birds at your feeders and take note of what they're eating or what they're tossing to the ground. Experiment with different blends and foods. For example, try adding softened raisins or dried cranberries to see if you attract a new species. Eventually, you'll find a couple of winning combinations that your backyard birds will love.

BACKYARD TIP
Regardless of whether you make or buy seed, store any bulk mixes tightly sealed in a cool, dark place.

DON'T attract unwanted guests.

Inexpensive store-bought seed blends can occasionally attract pesky visitors. They might contain red millet (white proso millet is a better option), wheat or other grain products that are typically used as filler. Avoid those things when creating your own birdseed mix and stick with quality seeds and foods.

DO buy supplies in bulk.

If you know you're going to use a lot of sunflower or safflower seeds while creating your homemade concoctions, buy the supplies in bulk. Membership big-box stores are great places to stock up and get a decent deal.

DON'T create a mess.

There are certain types of seed that are messier than others. Red millet, for example, often gets tossed to the ground by common songbirds, creating an even bigger mess than usual under your feeders. Even though sparrows, doves and cardinals

Providing different seed blends will attract cardinals, woodpeckers and more!

READER-TESTED, BIRD-APPROVED RECIPES
Our Birds & Blooms *field editors share their no-fail mixes.*

For a super simple seed combo, just incorporate black oil sunflower seed with cracked corn and plenty of peanuts.
Tiffany Ertle
HOMOSASSA, FLORIDA

This blend attracts so many birds—cardinals, blue jays, nuthatches, goldfinches and more! I combine safflower seeds, sunflower seeds, thistle, nuts, raisins and dried cranberries.
Kathy Lorigan
EASTON, PENNSYLVANIA

I buy cracked corn and black oil sunflower seed in bulk, store it in large plastic containers and then use an auger to mix the two seeds together as we need it. It saves money, and we only have to pay for the seed we want to serve the birds.
Kathy Eppers
ALEDO, TEXAS

WATER WORKS
Place a birdbath with a bubbler near flower containers in a small yard. Birds can't resist moving water!

Make Room for Birds

Turn your small backyard into a haven for feathered friends.
By Kirsten Sweet

Birds are easy to please. Give them the necessities—food, water and shelter—and they visit backyards of any size, or even balconies and patios, says Laura Erickson, bird expert and author.

Urban areas are as bird-friendly as large suburban backyards. Think about this: Most of our biggest cities are built on rivers or large lakes, which also happen to be migration pathways. As birds travel, especially during spring and fall migration, they're on the lookout for familiar scenery.

Jam-pack multiple containers with bird-friendly blooms and add a feeder and a birdbath, and your small space will be filled with birds in no time.

Get Spotted

The key to attracting birds to a small area is to get your space noticed, Laura says. And the first things a bird sees are plants, which they associate with food and shelter. Shrubs grow well in small yards or containers, and birds use them as nest sites or to escape from predators. Remember that plants are home to insects, which are an important part of a bird's diet. The more plants you have, the more birds you attract.

Select Super Seeds

Black oil sunflower seed is the go-to meal for virtually all birds, Laura says. It's an ideal option if you have space for only one feeder. Because the seeds are more fragile than striped sunflower, a variety of birds can crack them open easily.

Serve their favorite seeds in an acrylic window feeder if you are tight on space. Buy one with suction cups to attach to a pane of glass, and make sure it has tiny perches for songbirds, Laura says. The small perches prevent nuisance birds, like pigeons, from gaining access to the seeds.

Just Add Water

Get the biggest bang for your birdbath buck when you add moving water to an ordinary bath. Birds hear the trickling, bubbling sound and stop for a drink or a dip, Laura says. It can be as easy as adding a solar-powered pump to a bath in a sunny spot. Laura found that a desk bubbler placed in a shallow pan makes a simple water feature in a pinch.

Set up your backyard with the trifecta, and watch birds right from your window. Once birds find your space and adjust to the surroundings, they come back for more.

VICTORY IN THE CITY
Field editors share their best tips for feeding birds in urban areas.

I attach a board to the window ledge and sprinkle sunflower seeds across it. The birds come to the makeshift feeder even with me watching. The key is nearby shrubs that offer the birds protection.
Grace Huffman
OKLAHOMA CITY, OKLAHOMA

I have a feeding station and keep all the feeders together. Because I live in town, neighborhood cats are an issue, so the feeders are high up and near a tree to provide shelter for the birds.
Rebecca Williamson
BUSHNELL, ILLINOIS

FORGO A FEEDER

Spread white millet in front of shrubs for ground feeding birds, like juncos and sparrows. Or smear chunky peanut butter on a tree trunk for chickadees and woodpeckers.

A hungry young eastern bluebird is ready for its next meal.

More Bugs, More Birds

Grow beneficial plants to attract plenty of tasty insects, and watch the birds fly in to feast. **By David Mizejewski**

The key to increasing winged activity in your yard is in your plants. Native perennials, trees and shrubs offer a variety of natural foods, including seeds, berries, fruits, nuts, sap and nectar. The seed in feeders is only a supplement to the good eats birds get from natural landscapes. And having more plants means more of what birds need most—insects.

Bugs are especially important to birds during summer breeding season, when the parents need to feed hungry young broods. Right from the egg, hatchlings need the protein and fat insects provide to fuel their rapid growth. In fact, 96 percent of backyard birds rely on insects as a primary food source for their young.

Caterpillars, particularly moth caterpillars, are a vital source of food. And since they're more numerous than butterfly caterpillars, they aren't in danger

of being wiped out. Birds don't eat just a couple of caterpillars a day. Studies of chickadees show they may catch thousands of caterpillars during the 16 days it takes their babies to grow from hatching to fledging. A garden full of bugs is valuable to growing bird families.

There are other benefits to putting more of a focus on bug-friendly backyards. Some birds simply don't eat commercial seeds or are too shy to visit a busy feeder. A wealth of insects means more species will visit your yard. When

BEST-LOVED BUGS
Besides caterpillars, birds
eat these invertebrates:

Spiders	Grubs
Grasshoppers	Moths
Crickets	Flies
Beetles	

Yellow warbler

A chipping sparrow
feeds its hatchlings.

you supplement feeders with
plants, your yard keeps the bird
grub coming, even when you're
on summer vacation.

If you want birds, you've got to
have bugs, too, especially caterpillars.
Fill your yard with native plants,
focus on caterpillar host plants and
avoid insecticides. Rely on hungry
bird visitors to keep your insect
populations in check. When you
do, you'll be doing your part to
ensure that your favorite kinds
of birds will reproduce and keep
the species going.

Choose Natives
The National Wildlife
Federation plans to
launch a new tool to
help you use native
plants to support
insect populations.
Based on entomology
expert Doug Tallamy's
research, it will list
the best caterpillar
host plants native to
your ZIP code. To get
a list for your area,
visit *nwf.org/garden*.

DID YOU KNOW?
The male scarlet tanager (in a plum tree here) loses his bright red coloring in fall, molting to an olive green.

All About Tanagers

Discover the ins and outs of these four colorful migratory birds.

Western tanager

Scarlet Tanagers

His bright red body makes the male scarlet tanager easier to spot in the open, but unfortunately for birders, this tanager likes to forage for insects high up in deciduous canopies. Scarlet tanagers spend half the year in the Midwest and the Eastern parts of the U.S., migrating to South America for winter. Because scarlet tanagers are often forced to nest near open habitats due to deforestation, they are susceptible to brown-headed cowbirds that leave their eggs in tanager nests. **Attract scarlet tanagers to your yard with grape jelly and oranges.**

Western Tanagers

With his red-orange head, yellow body and black wings, the male western tanager looks like a little flame ball as he forages in coniferous forests for insects and berries. (The female's dull yellow coloring is less eye-catching.) As their name hints,

Hepatic tanager

these are the Western counterparts to scarlet tanagers. In summer, western tanagers can appear as far north as Southeastern Alaska—farther north than any other tanager species. **Attract them to your backyard with oranges, sugar water and native plants, which draw in bugs for tanagers to eat. Western tanagers have also been known to eat suet during cold snaps.**

Summer Tanagers

Watch out, bees! Although these brightly colored birds (males are a cardinal red and females mustard yellow) will eat most insects, their favorite meals are bees and wasps. Common in Southern woods full of oak trees, summer tanagers will catch wasps and rub them against branches to remove their stingers before eating them. Afterward, they'll eat the larvae left in the hive. **To coax summer tanagers to your yard, try leaving out sweet treats like blackberries and overripe bananas, which will attract bees, too.**

Hepatic Tanagers

Although hepatic tanagers are very widespread, trailing down as far as Argentina, they usually migrate north of the Mexican border only for the summer breeding season, during which they can be found in pine forests of the Southwestern U.S. **They eat mostly insects, such as beetles and caterpillars, but also enjoy berries, especially in late summer.** Hepatic tanagers get their name from the male's liverlike coloring.

TANAGER TALES
Readers share their snapshots and stories.

This photo of a western tanager was taken in one of my favorite hiking spots, Arthur's Rock Trail in Lory State Park near Fort Collins, Colorado. Usually I look overhead for birds hiding in trees, but this time, the tanager was at eye level—hard to miss with all his vivid colors.
Stephanie Montgomery
CORONA, CALIFORNIA

Summer tanager

My husband and I went to Ramsey Canyon Preserve near Sierra Vista, Arizona, for our anniversary last June, and while walking a trail, we came across this beautiful summer tanager sitting in the tree right in front of us.
Lisa Swanson
MARICOPA, ARIZONA

Blue Beauties

Follow these tips from our field editors, and you'll become a bluebird host in no time.

1

I use mealworms in a shallow, flat hanging feeder, and I always hang birdhouses on my deck rungs nearest the mealworms. Bluebirds seem to like that I put the food close to their nests. One season, we were lucky enough to have two broods. My best advice is to clean out the nest after their first brood so they return.
Kathy Lorigan
EASTON, PENNSYLVANIA

2

Keep an eye on the bluebird box. Wrens and sparrows might try to take it over. If other birds start nesting, I remove what they brought to the nest until they get sick of me. If you are lucky enough to have a nesting pair, you'll need to help the momma bluebird by watching the box to make sure sparrows stay away.
Connie Mason Etter
MARTINSVILLE, INDIANA

3

I built several bluebird houses and attached them to pine trees at the edge of my yard near woods. Every year I have many families, nests and babies. The birdbaths, the garden and many flower beds are nearby. I do put mealworms in the feeders, but I think the bluebirds just like my peaceful country yard.
Joan Heid
CHESTER, SOUTH CAROLINA

4

Offer a clean water source, preferably moving, to get their attention. Bluebirds love a good bath, and even a shallow dish in the shade will be a draw to families.
Laura Downing
PULASKI, TENNESSEE

5

Location is key. You need an open area, grass fields, water and cavities for nesting. Bluebirds are considered secondary-cavity nesters, which means they'll use natural cavities or cavities excavated by other species.
Boni Trombetta
WEST CHESTER, PENNSYLVANIA

Feed Your Finches

Boost your summer backyard space to attract even more eye-catching goldfinches.

It's hard to miss the cheerful yellow and contrasting black and white wing markings of male American goldfinches, especially when they're crowded around your backyard bird feeder. When winter arrives, the males take on a more subtle brown to match the females. If food is plentiful, American goldfinches won't typically migrate very far, which means their distinctive *per-chick-o-ree* call can be heard year-round.

At the Feeder

Goldfinches primarily eat seeds, which means they are big fans of bird feeders. Although goldfinches will eat most small seeds, they love thistle (Nyjer) and sunflower seeds. Keep goldfinches coming back by replacing uneaten food every three to four weeks. Make sure the seed stays dry. Most tube and mesh feeders are fine; a sock feeder also works well.

Sock thistle feeder

Around the Backyard

Seeds may be their food of choice, but goldfinches also occasionally enjoy the bark of young twigs, fresh tree buds and maple sap. Western red cedar, elm, birch and alder trees will encourage more goldfinches to stop by for lunch. In summer, goldfinches add a few small insects to their diets, but seeds remain at the top of the menu.

In the Garden

A few goldfinch favorites include asters, coneflowers, sunflowers and, of course, thistles. Goldfinches need plants for more than seeds: Milkweeds, cattails and dandelions provide fluffy nest-building material. One plant to avoid, however, is burdock, which has multiple burrs that can entangle the small birds.

Purple coneflower

blooming Beauty

Achieve the look you want in your yard. Focus on patterns to add interest, grow a fragrant flowering tree or plant a grouping of succulents. Our experts share tips on weeds, pruning and more.

garden WITH *patterns*

Your garden plants may not cruise the catwalk, but that doesn't mean they can't strut their stuff. Spikes, spirals, feathers, flames—there's a world of fashion ready to work it outside your back door. Does your garden need its own Project Runway? These plants add a punch of style worthy of Prada.

By Rachael Liska

Ball dahlia

COOL AND CONCENTRIC

Concentric design, when a series of circles or other shapes share the same center, fascinates and delights. These plants grab attention.

Ball Dahlia

This group of dahlias features petal-loaded compact flowers that look like a ball. They'll stop you in your tracks. A few favorites: Marble Ball, Boom Boom White, Cornel, Crichton Honey and Maarn. Zones 8 to 10, but treated as an annual in most areas of the country.

Camellia

Sunflower

Camellia
(Camellia japonica)
We're talking about the double bloomers—varieties like the hot pink Mathotiana Supreme and Nuccio's Bella Rossa (pictured above right). Looking for something more understated? Give sparkling white Nuccio's Gem a try. Hardy in Zones 7 to 10.

Sunflower
(Helianthus annuus L.)
A sunflower's head is made up of many tiny flowers called florets. The central florets follow a spiraling concentric pattern, which from a distance looks like the center of a normal flower. Close up? It's downright cool. Annuals thrive in Zones 4 to 9.

Maggie Daley astilbe blooms late in the season.

FLAMES AND FEATHERS

With striking shapes and sultry colors, these plants bring a touch of the exotic, and they are easy to incorporate into any garden style.

Astilbe

(Astilbe chinensis, Astilbe x *arendsii, Astilbe japonica)* Available in white, pink, red and plum hues, the plumes of airy astilbe bring sophistication to shady landscapes. Plant under trees or in front of foundation plants, where other plants often struggle to survive. Moist soil is key. Zones 4 to 8.

Durban Canna

(Canna x *generalis* 'Durban') No one can deny its orange-red blooms, but one look at its foliage and you'll know this variegated-leaf canna is hot stuff. Yellow veins decorate reddish-purple leaves, creating a smoldering effect. Leaves turn bronze as the season progresses. Zones 7 to 11.

Ornamental Grass

With feathery plumes, beautiful colors and airy growth habits, ornamental grasses offer four-season interest and movement in stagnant settings, making them the ultimate in low-maintenance gardening. Zones vary.

For a little tropical flair, add Durban canna to containers, flower beds, borders or water gardens.

Encore miscanthus

Freckle Face
blackberry lily

All-American
Magic rose

Part of the Winter
Jewels series,
Painted Doubles
is deer resistant.

SPOTS AND SPLATTERS

*You'll want these beauty marks to come back
to your perennial garden year after year.*

**Painted Doubles
Double Hellebore**
(*Helleborus* 'Painted
Doubles') A welcome
sight in very early spring,
its fluffy white blooms
are painted with red
brush-like marks and
add a dose of color to
a shady, winter-weary
garden. Zones 5 to 8.

**Trevi Fountain
Lungwort**
(*Pulmonaria* 'Trevi
Fountain') Sitting below
clusters of cobalt-blue
flowers that emerge in
spring, the silver-speckled
leaves steal the show. Plant
it along a shady pathway
or among a display of
spring-blooming bulbs.
Zones 3 to 9.

Blackberry Lily
(*Belamcanda chinensis*
'Freckle Face') Sporting
2-inch apricot blooms
flecked with reddish spots
and seed pods that look
like blackberries, these
plants look as good in
your garden as they do
in a vase. Zones 5 to 9.

**All-American
Magic Rose**
(*Rosa grandiflora*
'All-American Magic')
Big, bold and beautiful,
this rose has it all. Double
flowers emerge in bright
red and yellow stripes and
splatters, fading to pink
and cream. A great cut
flower, it's more disease
resistant than most striped
roses. Zones 6 to 9.

Trevi Fountain
lungwort

SPIKES AND SPIRALS

From edgy spikes to ethereal spirals, these shapes are full of drama and personality.

Sapphire Skies yucca

Yucca

(*Yucca* species and cultivars) Its swordlike leaves grow in a starburst pattern that sets it apart from ordinary garden plants. A few favorites: *Yucca rostrata* 'Sapphire Skies', *Yucca cernua* and *Yucca flaccida* 'Golden Sword'. Zones 4 to 11, depending on variety.

Prickly Pear

(*Opuntia*) Native to the Southwest, these interesting plants with clusters of spiky pads are becoming popular in Northern climates, too, where they make excellent container plantings. Zones 6 to 11.

Spiraled Rex Begonia

(*Begonia rex* hybrid) The snail shell-shaped foliage looks like something out of a fairy tale, which is why these begonia hybrids have gained in popularity, especially with container garden enthusiasts. Escargot, Curly Fireflush and Emerald Wave are exceptional cultivars.

Curly Fireflush rex begonia

Prickly pear cactus

STREAKS AND STRIPES

If your perennial garden looks more like a sea of green than a river of color, break up the boredom with plants that have earned their stripes.

Zebra Grass

(*Miscanthus sinensis* 'Zebrinus') As its name suggests, this exotic-looking ornamental grass features golden-yellow stripes on bright green blades. It's a wild one. Zones 5 to 9.

Circus Stripes iris

Circus Stripes Iris

(*Iris* 'Circus Stripes') Make a statement in springtime with majestic white blooms highlighted by deep purple edging and delicate veining. Zones 3 to 8.

June Hosta

(*Hosta* 'June') Beautiful, broad blue-green leaves streaked with creamy gold centers make this award-winning perennial a shady standout in any garden. Zones 3 to 9.

June hosta

BRANCH OUT
with blooms

Perk up spring landscapes with any of these 14 native flowering trees. **By Heather Lamb**

A prothonotary warbler perches in a native flowering dogwood tree.

for years,

I worked in an office with a window overlooking the woods. Each spring I'd watch as yellow daffodils emerged along its edge, but for me, the new season didn't start until I spotted the lone redbud in bloom. Its rose-pink glow amid the leafless trees felt like hope after a long winter.

Flowering trees often signal the return of spring. Combine that with the trees' typically smaller stature, and they are ideal for home landscapes. This list includes 14 suggestions, all North American natives.

Washington hawthorn

Desert willow trees are heat tolerant.

American plum
(Prunus americana)
This wild plum thrives across a huge swath of North America and occurs naturally in woodlands and along roadsides. Its fragrant white flowers emerge in early spring, followed by large, edible fruit. Left untended, it can become a thorny thicket, but it will grow upright with care. White flowers; 15 to 25 feet tall; Zones 3 to 8

Flowering crabapple
(Malus)
When I moved to Missouri, I was thrilled to discover a flowering crabapple in our new yard. The trees are abundant in Northern areas, but I'd never had one of my own. Lavish buds typically are pink when closed but open to white blooms. Crabapples were once plagued by disease, but dozens of cultivars now offer disease resistance as well as varied tree sizes and flower colors. White or pink flowers; 10 to 25 feet tall; Zones 4 to 8

Grow magnolia trees in Zones 5 to 9.

The showy blooms of a redbud tree are even more stunning when a northern cardinal stops for a visit.

Flowering dogwood
(Cornus florida)

If crabapple is the go-to choice for Northern gardeners, flowering dogwood is similarly sentimental in the South. The dogwood's low, horizontal branches and unmistakable flowers make it a classic, though it's not as plentiful as it once was because the trees aren't long-lived and are susceptible to disease. Plant in partial shade and moist, acidic and well-draining soil to keep the trees healthy. Pacific dogwood (*Cornus nuttallii*) is the species suited to the West Coast. White flowers; 20 feet tall; Zones 5 to 9 (*C. nuttallii*: 20 to 30 feet tall; Zones 7 to 9)

Sweetbay magnolia
(Magnolia virginiana)

The buds of sweetbay magnolia are less susceptible to frost because the tree blooms later in spring than its relatives. Once they emerge, the flowers live up to the family's reputation: They are creamy white, fragrant and large (2 to 3 inches). Native to areas prone to flooding, this magnolia often is multistemmed and remains relatively small. White flowers; 10 to 20 feet tall; Zones 5 to 9

Eastern redbud
(Cercis canadensis)

With deep pink blooms that glaze its leafless branches in early spring, and a low, horizontal form that is downright dashing, redbuds are a popular and versatile choice in Eastern gardens. A Western version called Greene California redbud (*Cercis orbiculata*) is similarly attractive. Rose-pink flowers; 20 to 30 feet tall; Zones 4 to 9

Washington hawthorn
(Crataegus phaenopyrum)

Although often grown for its fruit, this hawthorn variety is a worthy choice for its white spring flowers as well. (But fair warning: Many find the scent unpleasant. There are also thorns!) The tree grows into a broad oval shape and withstands heat better than other hawthorns. White flowers; 25 to 30 feet tall; Zones 4 to 8

Desert willow
(Chilopsis linearis)

A native of the Southwest, this tree tolerates heat but doesn't do well in wet conditions. Despite the name, the tree isn't part of the willow family; it's kin with catalpas and trumpet vines. The tree has multiple trunks

Downy serviceberry trees will flower as early as March.

147

American yellowwood has year-round interest.

An orchard oriole perches on Carolina silverbell.

and an airy habit. Its pink or white flowers open in late spring and continue through August. White or pink flowers; 15 to 25 feet tall; Zones 7 to 9

Downy serviceberry
(Amelanchier arborea)
Growing up, we called this tree a Juneberry, and my brother and I would join my mom in early summer to collect its fruit in old ice cream buckets. The downy is a good serviceberry selection for its ability to withstand varied soil types and conditions. The racemes of white flowers, though short-lived, are showy and appear in midspring. White flowers; 15 to 25 feet tall; Zones 4 to 9

American yellowwood
(Cladrastis kentukea)
With a spectacular late-spring display of pendulous panicles of fragrant white flowers, smooth gray bark and a broad, rounded crown, this is a striking focal tree. It's named for the bright yellow hue of its freshly cut wood. White flowers; 30 to 50 feet tall; Zones 4 to 8

Carolina silverbell
(Halesia carolina or *tetraptera)*
This tree rings in the spring season with silvery-white, bell-shaped flowers that dangle in pretty clusters. As its name suggests, the silverbell thrives in its native Southeast,

especially along waterways. In cool, moist and well-drained conditions, it's long-lived and easy to care for. White flowers; 30 to 40 feet tall; Zones 5 to 8

Tulip poplar
(Liriodendron tulipifera)
The leaves of this tree are tulip-shaped

Western soapberry

and the tree's flowers are tulip-like. The tree itself is grand in every way. It grows up to 90 feet tall. The flowers make an unforgettable impression with shades of yellow, orange and green. The tree grows quickly into a stately pyramidical form. It's also long-lived, with specimens hundreds of years old at former presidential

Tulip poplar trees grow quickly.

Fringe tree

flowering statements

Although many states selected evergreens as state symbols, flowering trees are well-represented among the ranks of official icons.

Arizona: palo verde
Delaware: American holly
Florida and South Carolina: cabbage palmetto
Hawaii: candlenut tree

Indiana, Kentucky and Tennessee: tulip poplar
Kansas and Nebraska: eastern cottonwood
Mississippi: magnolia
Missouri and Virginia: flowering dogwood

Ohio: Ohio buckeye
Oklahoma: eastern redbud
Wyoming: plains cottonwood

residences like Mount Vernon and Monticello. Yellow and orange flowers; 70 to 90 feet tall; Zones 4 to 9

White fringe tree
(Chionanthus virginicus)
The large, loose panicles of the fringe tree emerge in late spring and look like fluffy clouds dotting the tree's branches. Its botanical name is derived from the Greek words *chion* for snow and *anthos* for flower. This tree tolerates urban environments well and has an open, spreading habit and multiple trunks. White flowers; 12 to 20 feet tall; Zones 4 to 9

Western soapberry
(Sapindus drummondii)
Yellowish-white flowers in relaxed panicles emerge in late spring, followed by yellow-orange berries. Native to Texas, this tree is adaptable to varied soil conditions and grows to be equally tall and wide. The berries can get messy, and when crushed in water, they create suds. Yellow-white flowers; 25 to 30 feet tall; Zones 6 to 9

Common sassafras
(Sassafras albidum)
Though often recognized for its leaves, which can be three-lobed, single or mitten-shaped, this tree's flowers are just as distinctive. Yellow bunches of delicate flowers unfurl on a tree that grows into a handsome, rounded canopy. As a bonus, it has vibrant fall color. Yellow flowers; 30 to 60 feet tall; Zones 4 to 9

Wildlife, like this prairie warbler, depend on sassafras trees for food and shelter.

TOP 10

coleus favorites

Make room in your garden for
fast-growing, trouble-free coleus.
BY SALLY ROTH

Fishnet
Stockings

GARDEN TIP
Pinching off a few
inches from the tips
of stems, where
flower buds form, will
keep coleus plants
dense with leaves
and branches.

TOP 10

Today's selection of coleus, with countless leaf shapes and colors, no longer needs to hide in the shadows. Many varieties take front and center in sunny gardens, too. Coleus vary almost as much in size and growth habit as in color, and you can't tell just by looking at a starter plant in your hands. Check the label to see whether it will grow into tidy mounds for edging beds, trailing types to spill over containers, or statuesque giants for a powerful punch. This collection of 10 favorites is just the start of a new addiction to these easy, reliable plants.

attracts hummingbirds

▲ Kiwi Fern

Coleus leaves are a complicated mix of colors up close that meld into a single overall hue from farther away. That's the case with Kiwi Fern—the yellow edging of its burgundy leaves smudges into moody purple to warm brown to dull orange. Show off this upright, 12- to 24-inch-tall plant in sun to shade, with mounding plants at its feet.

Why we love it: Kiwi Fern blooms unusually heavily and unusually early. From July through September, its spikes of baby blue flowers attract hummingbirds, but you can also remove the blooms for a denser plant.

▲ Fishnet Stockings

Big and bold, this coleus can reach 3 feet tall, with an upright growth habit that's taller than wide. Play off its unusual markings with companions of simple, solid colors—lime and maroon ornamental sweet potato vines will make for a gratifying trio. Plant in shade to partial shade; although this one laughs at heat and humidity, it often sulks in full sun.

Why we love it: When grown in an old-fashioned black urn, the wide, veined leaves evoke the antique appeal of Victorian days, when coleus was the one of the new fads in gardening.

◀ Wizard Mix

An oldie but a goodie, this exuberant mix will yield all sorts of surprises. Just like a litter of kittens, you never know what colors you'll get. At about $5 for 100 seeds, one packet can fill an entire garden with mounded plants about 10 inches tall. Start seeds indoors, very early. A January sowing will yield dozens of good plants by May.

Why we love it: The first pair of "seed leaves" that sprout will be green, but then the fun begins! Colors and markings become evident, starting with the second pair of leaves, and get bolder and brighter as the plants grow.

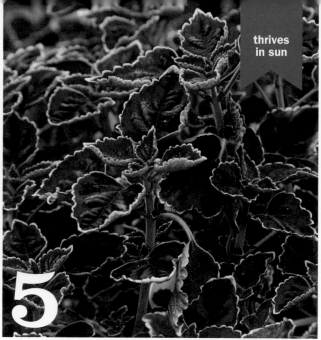

▲ Henna

The sharply serrated leaves of this 2-foot-tall by 2-foot-wide coleus look as if someone took scissors to the edges. Up close, they're golden chartreuse above and burgundy below. From a distance, the overall effect is warm copper.

Why we love it: The perfect contrast with blues and deep purples all summer, Henna is ideal for autumnal combinations, too. Try it with fountain grass and fall mums ranging from soft apricot to rich rusty tones.

▲ Trailing Plum

The absolute best cascading coleus, this low-growing, sun-loving variety is vigorous, graceful and gorgeous in containers. Avoid planting it in a terra-cotta pot, because the vivid purple will clash with the pot when the stems spill over the edge.

Why we love it: Trailing varieties of coleus are catching on fast; look for the word "trailing" in their names. Trailing Queen has classic neon pink-splashed leaves but in a whole new form.

▲ Black Dragon

Pink, green and white is a little old-school when it comes to coleus. Go for molten fire instead! At only about 12 inches tall and wide, Black Dragon is on the smaller side for coleus, but its look of bubbling, volcanic lava definitely stands out in the garden or in a container.

Why we love it: Dramatic Black Dragon can be started from seeds, which can be ordered online, or from cuttings. Sow seeds indoors 10 to 12 weeks before the last spring frost.

▲ Limelight

One of the Giant Exhibition coleus series, Limelight belies the name of its group: Its tidy mound is only 12 to 16 inches tall and wide. But, boy, is that color big! The near-neon leaves glow like a spotlight in shady spots and containers.

Why we love it: When it comes to combinations of colors, lime is nearly as versatile as a neutral. It goes with just about everything, including blues, purples, pinks, bright red or burgundy.

4 5: WHITE FLOWER FARM; 6 7 10: PARK SEED;

▲ Picture Perfect Salmon Pink

Keep this coleus in shade to part sun—say, in a large container on your porch—but echo its painterly colors in sunnier spots with soft apricot Dolce Flambe petunias, unusual brown weeping sedge (*Carex flagellifera*) or vivid Sunrise coneflower.

Why we love it: At 30 inches tall and wide, with extra-large leaves, this coleus is powerful enough to fill a container with a single plant. Seeds are available.

▲ Big Red Judy

Does your flower bed need something—but you're not sure what? Often it's calling for a dash of bold contrast, and Big Red Judy is just right. It's a giant, reaching 30 to 48 inches tall. Partner it with ornamental grasses, or let it glow among asters, black-eyed Susans, warm-colored coneflowers or any annuals.

Why we love it: Big Red Judy is Miss Congeniality: The soft, warm red goes with almost anything, and the simple leaves let fancier partners stand out.

snip for savings

Originally from the tropics, coleus plants (even the stoutest among them) will turn to mush when Jack Frost comes along: They're perennial only in Zone 11. Take cuttings before frost to enjoy their colors as houseplants over winter, and you'll have plants ready and waiting for next year, without spending a dime.

▲ Rustic Orange

Orange is the latest trend in gardening, and this gracefully branched, 18- to 24-inch-tall and -wide coleus is right on the mark. Use its unusual color to liven up dark neighbors, coleus or otherwise, in sun to shade. Or plant it next to pale apricot flowers to heighten their trendy effect.

Why we love it: The plain leaves create a dash of color that's irresistible to play with. Contrast that warm rusty orange with intensely blue annual lobelia for a simple classic. Or surprise the eye by partnering this versatile coleus with dark-throated magenta Shock Wave petunias.

Agave lophantha 'Quadricolor'

Smitten with

▶▶ EVEN SUPERSTAR PLANTS NEED A LITTLE TLC. HERE'S HOW TO

Kalanchoe luciae

Aeonium 'Sunburst'

Aloe plicatilis

Aloe distans

Succulents

GROW THEM WITH EASE. BY **HEATHER RAY** PHOTOS BY **DEBRA LEE BALDWIN**

Sedum rupestre 'Angelina'

Portulacaria afra 'Variegata'

Echeveria agavoides

SUCCULENTS have a supernatural ability to thrive in nearly any climate. From growing across rugged terrain in a sprawling desert to sprouting up inside a dainty teacup on a windowsill, these plants prove their toughness by storing water in fleshy leaves, fighting long periods of drought and producing new roots and rosettes. Today, the popularity of the desert dwellers arises from their resiliency, ease of propagation and exquisite formations.

Knowing what succulents like and dislike helps you understand when to tend to your near-invincible living works of art and when to let them be. Here are a few pointers to help you get growing.

Euphorbia tirucalli 'Sticks on Fire'

Crassula muscosa

Sedum nussbaumerianum 'Coppertone Stonecrop'

Aeonium urbicum

Kalanchoe tomentosa 'Golden Girl'

Sedum adolphii

Echeverias

FIND YOUR LOOK

Garden photojournalist Debra Lee Baldwin, author of *Succulent Container Gardens* and *Succulents Simplified*, attests that these plants can be grown anywhere by anyone. "Succulents are architectural and photogenic and have remarkable aesthetic aspects," Debra says. "Use them to express your style and creativity."

How you display them is a fundamental tenet of this type of gardening. Debra suggests containers that showcase the plant, referring to pots as the backup singers. She also recommends repeating design elements to create an overall soothing look, and playing with contrasting shapes, such as the glowing sunset colors of Sticks on Fire euphorbia (*Euphorbia tirucalli*) against an agave's blue-gray tones. In general, succulents grow well together in larger pots, but they are equally admirable in individual vessels. Adding to their list of secret superpowers, Debra says, they won't outgrow small containers, making them thoughtful accents for office or home windows.

Q: What's the difference between a cactus and a succulent?

A: Cacti are a type of succulent, which simply means having leaves or stems capable of storing water.

PLANT FOR SUCCESS

Succulents, which include cacti, grow in both nondraining and draining containers. For pots with no holes, you may be tempted to add a layer of rocks to the bottom to create a drainage layer. While this sounds good in theory, Debra advises against it. "This is a common fallacy," she says. "That layer of rocks provides an area for bacteria to grow." Under watering is actually a better solution. Use well-aerated soil designed for succulents and cacti, as regular soil with a higher peat content will hold too much water. And if you're worried about soil seeping out of pots with holes, slap on some mesh tape. Once you have the plants all tucked in, top the soil with pebbles or gravel for a finished look.

PREPARE FOR WINTER

Where your plants prefer to winter depends on whether they are soft (also called tender) or hardy varieties. Some soft types tolerate temperature dips into the mid-20s (about Zone 9), whereas other varieties are less forgiving when exposed to below-freezing winters. Aeonium, aloe, crassula, echeveria, jade, kalanchoe and senecio are common frost-tender types.

For indoor growing, select a bright location, preferably near a south or east window. Your windowsill makes a lovely perch, but check to make sure the plants aren't getting too much sun; believe it or not, even sun lovers can get scorched, especially if they're young and newly planted. "The concern is that UV rays, magnified by window glass, may sunburn the leaves," Debra says.

Hardy forms, however, are less worrisome for outdoor gardeners and withstand cold and frost down to Zone 5. Some varieties even survive in Zones 3 and 4. Popular hardy varieties include jovibarba, sedum, opuntia and sempervivum.

WATER RESPONSIBLY

The No. 1 secret to caring for succulents is to not overwater them. Give them a good soak and then wait for the soil to nearly dry out. Remember, succulents don't like damp environments and will likely rot if their container is routinely saturated.

How often you water is contingent on the type of plant and time of year. During their growing season in spring and summer, they are a tad thirstier, but come fall and winter, they go practically dormant and need very little water. And keep in mind, nondraining containers, such as Mason jars and stone mugs, require lighter showers.

Once you start experimenting with the endless style combinations that succulents have to offer, don't be surprised if you start rummaging through garage sales or thrift shops in search of interesting vessels. It's nothing more than a sign you've become smitten with succulents. Welcome to the club.

This kalanchoe, also known as paddle plant, pairs nicely with blue echeveria.

⇥ 5 Quick Fixes

Debra Lee Baldwin, known as the Queen of Succulents, shares her best troubleshooting tips.

PROBLEM: Bleached, beige or dark spots on leaves.
CAUSE: Too much sun.
SOLUTION: Move into bright shade.

PROBLEM: Puffy or squishy stems.
CAUSE: Too much water.
SOLUTION: If the roots are dead, take clippings from healthy tissue and replant in new soil.

PROBLEM: Collapsed, mushy leaves.
CAUSE: Frost.
SOLUTION: Cover plants or move indoors until the temperature rises.

PROBLEM: Stretched stems and leaves.
CAUSE: Not enough light.
SOLUTION: Adjust the location.

PROBLEM: Loss of shine; shriveled tips.
CAUSE: Not enough water.
SOLUTION: Keep soil only as dry as a wrung-out sponge.

Pink Butterflies kalanchoe will grow in sun to light shade.

Build a prairie garden full of black-eyed Susans and other natives. Your space will be low-maintenance and wildlife-friendly.

grow your
own grassland

**Bring the prairie home
with colorful native
plants that wildlife love.**

By Sheryl DeVore

Bee balm

a tiger swallowtail butterfly sips nectar from bee balm's purple blooms. A goldfinch snatches seeds from a black-eyed Susan. Indiangrass sways in the wind. Whether you have a large space or a small one, you can re-create this native prairie scene in your backyard.

Prairie plants save time and money because, once mature, they require no fertilizer and no watering. "They're part of an ecosystem that keeps water clean and soils healthy, while providing native animals great habitat," says Laura Jackson, executive director of the Tallgrass Prairie Center at the University of Northern Iowa in Cedar Falls.

Prairie plants also are part of our national heritage, and it's important we do all we can to save them. Shortgrass and tallgrass prairies once covered 600,000 square miles of North America. Now, less than 1 percent of native tallgrass prairie remains, Laura says.

Although you can start a prairie garden in spring, fall is a fantastic time, too, because that's when seeds mature and scatter. Before you start, check local ordinances regarding height and location limitations of yard plants. Ask other gardeners if they have seeds to share, and don't forget to pay it forward when your own prairie becomes established.

STEP ONE: Pick the Plants

Conservation areas and forest preserves sell native prairie plants in spring and fall. In autumn, gardeners often sponsor seed and transplant exchanges. "Just don't buy a prairie in a can, and if you go to a garden center, make sure you're buying straight species, not cultivars," Laura says. Go online or reach out to local nature centers to learn which wildflowers, called forbs, and grasses grow best where you live.

Potted flowers and grasses are good bets. They may be more expensive and need water the first year or two, but they help establish your prairie garden quicker than seeds, which can be eaten by wildlife before they have a chance to germinate.

Select species that don't grow much taller than 3 or 4 feet—perhaps 50 percent native grasses like little bluestem and 50 percent forbs such as bee balm and black-eyed Susan. In a few years, experiment with taller forbs and grasses.

STEP TWO: Choose the Spot

Give prairie plants what they want: lots and lots of sun. Pick a spot away from trees and other tall vegetation that could cast shade. Decide how much lawn or other vegetation you want to convert to a native prairie garden. Remember: Start small and expand later.

It's important to properly prep the area you've chosen. Benjamin Vogt, owner of Monarch Gardens, a landscape firm in Nebraska, started his prairie garden by removing part of his lawn. He cut sod into 1½-inch-deep strips with a shovel. Then he removed them, mulched the area and planted immediately. You can do as he did, or place a tarp on the lawn and weigh it down for about a month until the grass has died, although this may kill some beneficial microorganisms. Rake up any debris, then plant. Both methods can be done in either spring or fall.

STEP THREE: Start Digging

For seeds, use an 8-ounce cup of seed per square meter. Spread native grass seeds first, lightly raking the seed into the soil. Then scatter the wildflower seeds but do not rake them in. Scattering seeds just before it snows protects them from hungry birds. Some prairie seeds need to overwinter in the cold before they can germinate.

For established plants and seedlings, place tags by each one so you won't accidentally dig them up when weeding. Water as you would any other perennial. If you want to use seeds and established plants, scatter the seeds first.

STEP FOUR: Maintain Your Prairie

New seedlings only grow a few inches in their first year. But mow taller weeds back to about 6 inches to keep them in check. After you've done this several times, you can stop. In colder climates, let snow blanket the seeded areas, wait for seedlings to pop up in spring, and follow the same mowing method. For transplants, keep the area weeded and water when necessary the first year or two.

Although some gardeners cut down stems and stalks of wildflowers and grasses after bloom time, leaving them up through the seasons provides food for birds and other wildlife. About every three years, mow your patch down to soil level in spring and rake off debris. Many grasses and forbs have deep root systems, so they will survive a mowing.

It might take several years for your prairie garden to look nice, so be patient. Also note that some plants spread like crazy—black-eyed Susan, for example. Just dig them up and share with your neighbors. Keep shrubs and trees in check so they don't shade out your prairie garden.

STEP FIVE: Sit Back and Enjoy

A prairie garden is a mix of interesting leaves, buds, flowers and seeds visited by hummingbirds, moths, bees, butterflies and birds. In fall, grasses in some climates turn shades of gold, orange, and bronze, while finches and other birds perch on dead blossoms to eat nutritious seeds. Depending on weather and other factors, each season brings different sights and sounds to your prairie garden.

10 TO GROW ON

Check out these flowering plants and grasses. (They can grow up to 4 feet tall!)

1. Pale purple coneflower *(Echinacea pallida)*
2. Wild bergamot or bee balm *(Monarda fistulosa)*
3. Indiangrass *(Sorghastrum nutans)*
4. Common milkweed *(Asclepias syriaca)*
5. Gray-headed coneflower *(Ratibida pinnata)*
6. Little bluestem *(Schizachyrium scoparium)*
7. Black-eyed Susan *(Rudbeckia hirta)*
8. Blazing star *(Liatris spicata)*
9. New England aster *(Aster novae-angliae)*
10. Prairie dropseed *(Sporobolus heterolepis)*

Plant perennial wildflowers instead of a typical lawn for a healthy green space.

9 STEPS TO GROWING A

» Adopt earth-friendly habits and your yard

GREENER BACKYARD

(and wallet) will thank you. **By Rachael Liska**

IT PAYS TO BE GREEN, whether it's because you want to live an environmentally conscious lifestyle or you simply want to save time and money. No matter your motives, your backyard will be better for it. Here are a few tips for transforming your space from good to great.

1

DON'T MOW AS DEEP. Try letting your lawn grow a few inches to help it better tolerate drought conditions in warmer months. (Cool-season grasses can grow up to 3½ to 4 inches, while most warm-season grasses are shorter.) Roots grow deeper and lawns thicker, which means fewer pests, less disease and a decreased need for chemical intervention.

2

GROW LOCAL. Native plants are accustomed to their area's growing conditions, so they're a smart low-maintenance option. Once established, they generally require less water and have fewer pest and disease problems. Native wildlife love them, too, as they're a fantastic source of food and shelter. Check with your local nursery or extension service to see which species are appropriate for the growing conditions in your neck of the woods.

The best compost is equal parts of carbon-rich and nitrogen-rich waste.

Build time into your morning routine for watering plants.

3

WATER THE RIGHT WAY. Water between 6 and 10 a.m., when the air is cool and not as much moisture will be lost to evaporation. Watering in late afternoon is the next best option. Be sure that foliage has time to dry before damp nighttime temperatures (and fungal diseases) set in. Water near the base of plants rather than overhead—soaker hoses are ideal, as they save water by slowly delivering the good stuff right to the roots. For lawns, water long and deep (an inch should do) once a week.

4

GET KEEN ON COMPOSTING. It's not called "gardener's gold" for nothing. Compost keeps kitchen leftovers out of landfills and enriches soil with much-needed nutrients. Not only does it reduce dependency on chemical fertilizers, it also improves drainage, water retention and soil texture. Veggie and fruit scraps, tea bags, coffee grounds, eggshells, dry leaves, shredded newspaper and untreated grass clippings are all fair game. *birdsandblooms.com/ gardening/gardening-basics/composting*

5

OPT FOR OUTDOOR FURNITURE THAT'S EARTH-FRIENDLY.

When shopping for wood benches or tables, check to make sure they are certified as sustainable. A hardwood like acacia, which grows in abundance and is considered invasive in many regions, and wood such as teak, from plantations managed for long-term preservation, are good choices. The same goes for patio sets made from recycled aluminum or plastic.

6

SAVE WITH SOLAR LIGHTING.

Make the backyard as beautiful in the dark as it is in the daytime with night-lights. With solar-powered spotlights, deck lights and path lights available in various sizes, it's easy to find a style that suits your landscape. They don't need wires or extension cords, so you can put them in any sunny spot.

6. Cut energy use with solar lamps.

9. Bee balm is a pollinator magnet for attracting bees, butterflies and more.

7

GROW TO BE WILD.

Trade in the mower for some mulch. Take a corner of your lawn and replace it with a bed of pretty native plants or mulch that can be used to anchor a kids play set. Plant a fairy garden full of frilly ferns in an area that receives a lot of shade, or try a rain garden in a low-lying spot of waterlogged lawn. Living in the desert? Use cactus and stone to build a water-efficient xeriscape.

8

MULCH FALL LEAVES WITH YOUR MOWER.

Forget all that raking, blowing and bagging. Let fall leaves lie, and cut them into tiny bits with a mulching lawn mower instead. This saves your back, and the shredded leaves add nutrients to the soil as they decompose. Shred leaves when grass is poking through them (don't let the leaves bury the grass completely). If you don't have a mulching mower, look into a leaf vacuum with mulching capabilities.

9

ROLL OUT THE RED CARPET TO POLLINATORS.

According to the U.S. Fish & Wildlife Service, pollinators such as honeybees, butterflies and hummingbirds help pollinate 75 percent of our flowering plants and nearly 75 percent of our crops. There is increasing evidence that many of these vital pollinators are in decline. Planting a garden that includes plants that flower at different times of the year will provide nectar and pollen sources for pollinators throughout the growing season. Whenever possible, choose native plants in a variety of flower colors and shapes. See *fws.gov/pollinators* for more information.

keep 'em

Japanese painted fern

WHY YOU NEED TO PUT A LITTLE DISTANCE BETWEEN CERTAIN PLANTS IN YOUR GARDEN. By Niki Jabbour

Purple coneflower

SEPARATED

It's a fact; not all plants play well together. Perhaps they're competing for sunlight, nutrients or water, or maybe they attract the same pests and diseases. Whatever the reason for keeping some plants apart, doing a little homework before you head to the nursery can save you a lot of time, frustration and money.

FIGHTING FLOWERS

Nancy Ondra, author of *The Perennial Matchmaker: Create Amazing Combinations with Your Favorite Perennials*, says there are a few factors that affect the compatibility of potential perennial partners, including preferred growing conditions and relative vigor. But a bad combination isn't the end of the world. You can easily dig up and move the incompatible plants.

Nancy points out that growing plants out of their comfort zone can induce stress, which reduces the amount and size of blooms, and results in weak stems that require staking. It also makes the plants vulnerable to pests and diseases.

"Some popular perennials are quite adaptable; for instance, you can sometimes get away with pairing a sun-loving perennial, such as purple coneflower, with one that normally prefers the shade, like Japanese painted fern," she says. "Your best bet is to avoid matching those with distinctly different needs, and instead pick partners that share the same light, soil and climate preferences."

SICKLY COMPANIONS

When teaming up plants, think about more than plant size, flowering period and color; also consider potential problems. For example, perennial favorites like garden phlox and bee balm are both prone to powdery mildew, a fungus that coats the leaves in a white powder. The affected foliage is unsightly, and the fungus can cause leaves to fall off. Planting two mildew prone plants side by side is inviting trouble.

Instead, pick cultivars that show resistance. A 2011 study at the Chicago Botanic Garden identified Shortwood, Candy Floss and Goldmine varieties of garden phlox as highly resistant to powdery mildew.

Spotted dead nettle

Hosta

DO pair up plants with similar growing rates. Spotted dead nettle needs a partner like hosta, which can hold its own next to a speedy grower and won't be overtaken.

Bee balm

Garden phlox

PERENNIAL PROBLEM-MAKERS

The phrase "ground cover" is often code for "aggressive plant," a lesson that Tara Nolan, the author of *Raised Bed Revolution*, has learned well. She advises no more than one spreading plant per bed.

"My sweet woodruff and catmint are planted beside each other and are hard to contain," Tara says. "The sweet woodruff is especially problematic as it has started to poke up through everything, even my nearby ice plant."

Perennial expert Nancy suggests doing a little research before you tuck spreading plants into your garden.

"Unbalanced growth rates can certainly result in poor perennial partners," Nancy warns. "It's easy for an enthusiastic spreader such as spotted dead nettle to crowd out a more restrained bedmate, such as dwarf bleeding heart." She advises selecting an equally sturdy partner for a spreading plant like the spotted dead nettle—a hosta, for instance.

ALLELOPATHY

Anyone who has tried to grow certain plants under a black walnut tree will understand the impact that allelopathy can have on plants. Allelopathic plants produce natural chemicals that can prevent seed germination or inhibit growth of nearby plants. In black walnuts, the toxic compound is called juglone, and is produced in the leaves, roots, fruit and branches. Juglone-sensitive plants, like rhododendrons, peonies, potentilla, privet, potatoes and tomatoes, will suffer if planted near black walnut trees. Instead, look for plants that tolerate juglone: daffodils, daylilies and hostas.

Other members of the walnut family, including butternut, as well as common garden plants like sunflowers, can be toxic to nearby plants. Bird lovers may notice that few plants grow beneath their sunflower seed feeders—that's allelopathy at work.

Daylily

Black walnut tree

HAPPY TOGETHER

Who says edibles and ornamentals can't grow side by side? I call them "garden BFFs": I enjoy tucking decorative vegetables into my flower borders and annual flowers into my vegetable patch. Here are three reasons why.

BEAUTY

There are countless vegetables and herbs with attractive foliage, flowers or fruits, making them good choices for ornamental gardens. Try edging your perennial border with curly parsley, leaf lettuce or Spicy Globe basil, or add clumps of Peppermint Swiss chard to your container gardens or flower beds.

BETTER YIELD

Planting pollinator-friendly annuals (cosmos, nasturtiums, zinnias) in your vegetable garden attracts bees and other pollinators. This means better pollination for flowering edibles (cucumbers, squash, strawberries), which in turn means bigger yields.

PEST PREVENTION

I always include plants that are attractive to beneficial insects like parasitic wasps and hover flies. These voracious hunters will reduce the populations of common pests like aphids. Try dill, sweet alyssum, fennel and coriander.

QUARRELING CROPS

There are several reasons to keep certain crops apart. Perhaps they attract the same pests and diseases, use up the same nutrients or have different needs. You may also want to consider crop size when matching vegetables. For example, a tall crop like corn or trellised peas will cast a shadow that might impact the growth of neighboring sun-loving crops like peppers, tomatoes, squash or cucumbers.

KISSING COUSINS

To boost yield, many gardeners practice intercropping, when a short-season crop needs to be grown in the same space and at the same time as a long-season crop. When the former is harvested, the latter has more room to grow. However, not all vegetables make good neighbors, and certain plants should be separated. For example, you can grow vegetables in the same family near each other, but you should not plant them as intercrops. Not only are they vulnerable to the same pests and diseases, they have similar fertility needs. This can deplete soil nutrients and hurt plant growth and yield.

DO put veggies next to annuals that will attract butterflies and bees. The edible crops will flourish with the attention.

If planting large space-hogging crops like cabbages, pumpkins and cauliflower, try intercropping with radishes, which can be harvested before the larger crops run out of room.

DROUGHT VS. DELUGE

You'll have a more successful garden if you keep crops with differing cultural needs away from each other. Celery and celeriac, for example, are water hogs, demanding regular, deep irrigation. Pepper plants, on the other hand, originated in Central and South America, where they got plenty of heat, with modest, consistent watering. Planting celery next to red peppers will mean you'll have either thirsty celery with stunted, fibrous stalks, or waterlogged peppers with drooping leaves and poor overall health. Instead, plant these crops near others with similar needs. Peppers grow well next to eggplant, basil or tomatoes. Celery and celeriac enjoy the company of cauliflower or leeks.

Peppermint Swiss chard

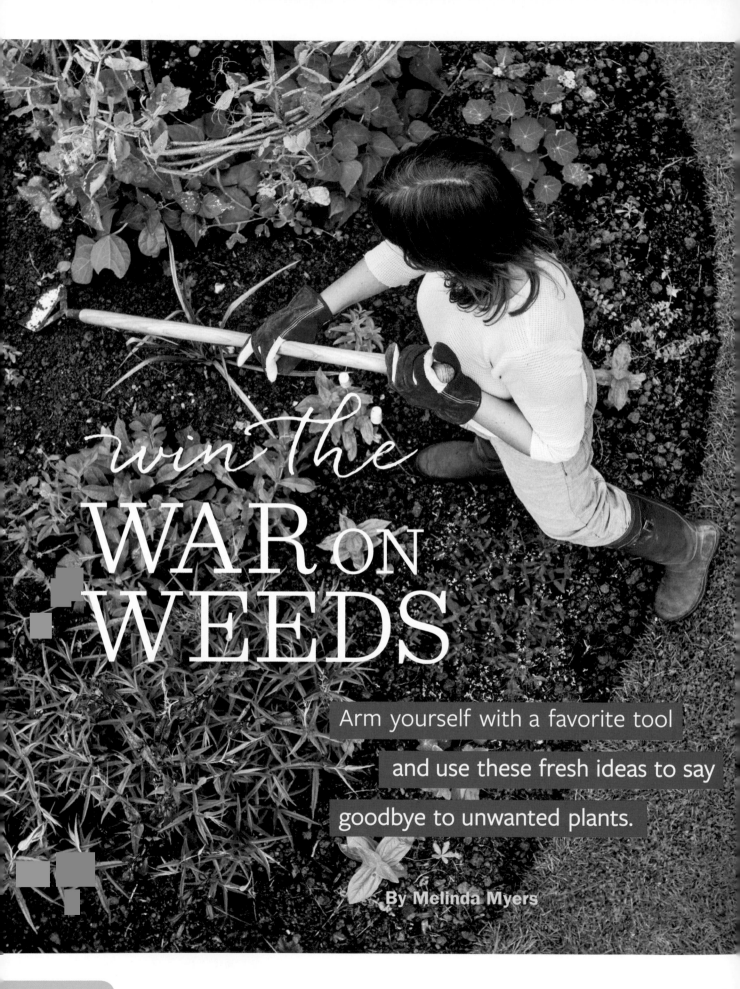

win the WAR ON WEEDS

Arm yourself with a favorite tool and use these fresh ideas to say goodbye to unwanted plants.

By Melinda Myers

With a new outlook and a little elbow grease, you can more efficiently weed out undesirable plants and even have fun doing it. Whether you transform the chore into a party or hit the garden instead of the gym, these tips and tricks pave the way for a weed-free backyard.

1 Change your mind-set. Pulling weeds is a stress reliever and workout because the movements stretch and strengthen muscles. Plus, you burn as many as 200 calories in 30 minutes. When you're finished, your blood pressure is lower and your mood improved.

2 Keep supplies handy. If tools and gloves are nearby instead of buried in a shed, it's easier to tackle the yard. Stash a bucket with favorite weeding tools at each entryway and garage door. Or give an old mailbox new life as a convenient place to store supplies right in the garden.

3 Make use of spare moments. Pluck a few dandelions while you're waiting for a ride, when dinner is in the oven or during a short break from another garden task. Take on one small section at a time, and before you know it an overwhelming job becomes manageable.

4 Pull throughout the season. The smaller the weeds, the simpler they are to remove. Getting them out of the garden before they go to seed prevents hundreds, or even thousands, of offspring next year.

5 Time it right. Yank 'em when soil is slightly moist and soft, and the pesky plants will be effortless to remove, roots and all. Soil that is soaked is easily damaged when you walk on it, dig in it or cultivate it, but when it's dry, roots get left behind and may eventually sprout—and must be pulled again later.

6 Remove annual weeds on a sunny day. As you move from one area to the next, leave seedlings on the soil surface so they quickly dry and die. As long as they haven't gone to seed, add them to a compost pile or use them as mulch around other plants.

7 Find a tool you love. Long-handled hoes and cultivators are kinder to your body, minimize your time spent bending over and help conserve your energy, so you can cover more ground. Use a single-prong cultivator to carefully reach around desirable plants. To remove plants deeply rooted in the landscape, try a weed digger or garden knife.

8 Add mulch to prevent unwanted seeds from sprouting. Make it extra beneficial by using materials from your garden. Spread a layer of herbicide-free grass clippings, shredded leaves or evergreen needles over the soil surface. Besides suppressing weeds, the material also conserves moisture and gives soil a boost as it breaks down. To stop difficult plants, put a layer of newspaper or cardboard down first and cover with mulch.

9 Throw a gardening round-robin party: Invite friends and neighbors to take turns tending each other's gardens. (This is also a fun way to swap tips or plants.) Start with coffee and tea in the first garden, then celebrate the end of a full day of weeding with a potluck dinner or a wine and cheese get-together.

10 Plan, plan, plan. It's possible to get ahead of weeds with good preparation and planting. Do some research for next spring and be sure to grow the right plant in the right location. You'll be rewarded with stronger, healthier plants that outcompete the unwanted plants.

11 Enhance soil with compost. Spread a 1-inch layer of compost over the soil surface of established perennial gardens. Use an auger bit to drill holes several inches deep throughout the garden bed. Top-dress with compost and aerate for stronger plants, beautiful flowers and a more productive vegetable garden.

12 Call on chemicals. If you're at a loss and decide to use chemicals, read and follow all label directions. Organic products made from soaps, vinegars and plant oils burn off the tops of plants, so perennial weeds may come back. If needed, try a total vegetation killer that contains glyphosate and destroys roots. Remove the bottom of a milk jug, set the jug over an individual plant, and spray (do this with organic or synthetic products to protect nearby plants). Allow it to dry before moving on.

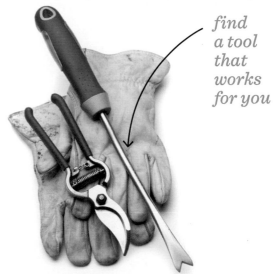

find a tool that works for you

Think of garden tasks as exercise. You can burn up to 200 calories in 30 minutes of weeding.

BECOME A PRUNING
pro

Get the job done right
with advice from an
experienced gardener.

By Niki Jabbour

TOP TOOLS
*Use hand pruners when
removing stems less than
¾ inch thick. Bypass
pruners are preferred
because they result
in a clean cut.*

f or most deciduous trees and shrubs,
winter is the best time for pruning. Plants are dormant and bare, so it's easier to see the branching structure and get a sense of what needs to be removed. It's also better for the plant because winter pruning promotes quick regrowth in spring and limits the exposure of the wound to insects and disease.

The first rule of pruning is this: Don't prune unless you have a good reason. One reason could be the appearance. You might have a young plant like a fruit tree, and want to train it into an open canopy and balanced shape. Or maybe you want to control the size of a shrub to ensure it doesn't outgrow its space. A major reason for pruning is to encourage flowering or increase fruit production, especially in plants like forsythia and highbush blueberry. Finally, dead, broken or hanging branches are a safety hazard, so it's best to get them out of the way.

Pruning can be an intimidating task for a lot of gardeners, but pruning mistakes are similar to a bad haircut: It may look funny for a while, but it'll grow back. Here are some tips to help you tackle winter pruning.

PREVIOUS SPREAD, FROM LEFT: GARY BLAKE/ALAMY STOCK PHOTO; LINDA BURGESS/GETTY

PRUNE AND SHAPE
To keep vining plants like this climbing hydrangea looking great, use pole pruners for hard-to-reach spaces.

Use a lopper tool for stems up to 1¾ inches thick.

DOs

DO pick a dry, sunny day, which is more comfortable for you and beneficial for the plant. Wet plants can spread disease.

DO start with clean, sharp tools. If you remove diseased tissue, wipe your pruning tools with a 10 percent bleach solution between cuts.

DO study the shape of the plant and consider each cut before you prune.

DO start by removing the three D's—any dead, damaged or diseased wood.

DO take out any crossing branches. Rubbing injures plant tissue and invites disease. Typically, the smaller of the two branches is removed.

DO remove water sprouts and suckers. Suckers grow from the base of the trunk or the roots of trees, while water sprouts emerge from branches. Both are vigorous, fast-growing shoots, but interfere with healthy growth, flowering and fruiting. Water sprouts on fruit trees also block air and sunlight, reducing fruiting and increasing the risk of wounds and disease.

DO trim long, unbranched stems back to a healthy, outward-facing bud. This is called heading and will stimulate nearby side buds and branches to grow.

DO prune overgrown or bushy trees and shrubs by making thinning cuts, the most common type of cut. This will allow more light and air to reach the center of the plant. To thin, prune the branch or stem back to its point of origin at the base of the plant, a main stem or the trunk.

DO take frequent breaks to step back and study the plant to make sure your pruning looks balanced and natural.

What to prune in winter

• Summer-flowering shrubs and trees such as rose of Sharon, crape myrtle, potentilla, smoke bush, butterfly bush and beautyberry. They produce flower buds on new growth and respond well to dormant pruning in winter. Shrubs grown for foliage, such as barberry, privet and burning bush, are also good candidates for winter pruning.

• Deciduous fruit trees such as apples, pears, cherries and plums. Dormant pruning removes some of the flower buds, but it also opens up the tree to more light and air, boosting tree health and fruit size and quality.

• Fruiting shrubs such as highbush blueberries, currants and gooseberries. Remove the oldest stems at ground level to encourage fresh fruiting branches.

• Deciduous trees like oak, honey locust and linden. As with smaller shrubs and trees, it's easier to see the framework of the branches in the winter.

What not to prune in winter

• Spring-flowering shrubs and trees like forsythia, lilac, quince, bigleaf hydrangea, rhododendron and azalea, which form their flower buds on wood from the previous year. These are best pruned after flowering in spring.

• Trees with heavy winter sap flow like maples, dogwoods and birches. Sap loss won't hurt the trees, but it can make a sticky mess on nearby structures, cars or furniture. These trees are easier to prune in midsummer when sap flow isn't a problem.

• Most conifers should be pruned during their growth spurt in late spring. Do research on specific conifers for tips.

TOUGH TREES
Flowering dogwoods and other trees require a pruning saw to manage branches that are too large for hand pruners or loppers.

DON'Ts

DON'T leave unsightly stubs, which can become diseased or infested with insects. Instead, prune to a healthy out-facing bud or branch.
DON'T shear shrubs into unnatural shapes unless you wish to create a formal hedge or topiary. Trees and shrubs look best when allowed to grow to their natural shape and size.
DON'T overprune. A rule of thumb is to remove no more than a fourth to a third of the canopy per year.
DON'T be shy about pruning mature neglected shrubs. Multistemmed shrubs like lilacs, forsythias and dogwoods can be rejuvenated with

the gradual removal of old wood. Begin by pruning a fourth to a third of the old stems. Repeat each year until all the old wood is removed.
DON'T cut tree limbs flush to the trunk. Instead, cut the branch where it meets the branch collar. This will promote quick and healthy callusing of the wound and there is no need for pruning paint.
DON'T forget safety! Wear eye protection. Never prune plants close to power lines or try to remove branches that can't be reached with a pole pruner. Instead, call the experts!

Drought-Tolerant Gardening

Conquer the challenges of a blooming backyard in the Southwest and other dry regions.

TROUBLESHOOTING THE SOIL

Arid soil tends to have high pH and low organic matter, but native drought-tolerant plants have adapted to these types of soil. Adding compost and overfertilizing can lead to root rot and floppy growth, whereas mulching conserves moisture and suppresses weeds. Take your cue from Mother Nature and consider rocks and gravel where appropriate. Doing so will also help prevent soil erosion.

CHOOSING THE RIGHT PLANTS

When it comes to maintaining a garden successfully in an arid environment, drought-tolerant native plants are key. Think blooming cacti, such as Santa Rita prickly pear, and tough succulents like agave. For color, try red yucca or firecracker penstemon (a hummingbird favorite). Not only can these plants survive and thrive in full desert sun, they can also withstand freezing night temperatures. Check with the local extension service for a list of the plants that will grow best in your area.

DEALING WITH DROUGHT

It's easy to take a wrong turn when watering a desert garden, either watering too much or too little. To make sure your plants get the optimal amount of water, set up drip irrigation, which allows moisture to seep slowly into the soil to the roots. A drip irrigation system can be as simple as a punctured garden hose or milk jug. (See *birdsandblooms.com/blog/diy-drip-water-plants-using-milk-jugs.*) Desert gardens can be tricky, but with the right resources and know-how, you'll be coaxing greenery out of yours in no time.

MORE DROUGHT-TOLERANT PLANT OPTIONS TO TRY

- Yellow columbine
- Bunny ears cactus
- Indian paintbrush
- Green-flowered hedgehog cactus
- Russian sage
- Texas blue sage
- Parry's agave
- Wine cup
- Agastache

Container DOs and DON'Ts

*Tips for a thriving small-space garden from the
National Garden Bureau.*

DO select a container that will give your plants' roots room to grow, but not so much space that they will not fill out the pot when mature.

DO plant in pots with drainage holes. Some decorative containers might not have drainage holes. If so, drill a few holes yourself or place a smaller pot inside the decorative one to give water a place to drain. Elevate the inner pot on stones, so water will collect at the bottom of the larger container.

DON'T use soil directly from the garden. As tempting as it is to dig up some backyard dirt and throw it into a container, potted plants need drainage. Look for potting mixes that have vermiculite, peat moss, compost, perlite or a combination.

DON'T pat the soil down after scooping it into the pot. Looser soil is easier on the roots.

DON'T forget to mulch. Pots in full sun will benefit from a layer of mulch to help the soil retain moisture and discourage weeds.

DO stake tall plants. Vining plants such as morning glories and tomatoes will need a stake or small trellis for support. Add the support right when you plant so you don't disturb the roots later.

DO use containers to experiment with planting in different parts of your yard. Try a new plant on a small scale, or test a shady spot to see how well certain plants will perform with little sun.

*Angelonia
(thriller)*

*Sweet potato
vine (spiller)*

*Diamond Frost
euphorbia (filler)*

TRY THIS!
Once you've got a thriller, spiller and filler, add more favorites, like the yellow lantana shown here.

glad you asked!

Gardening expert Melinda Myers answers your questions.

A Double Play pink spirea from Proven Winners can be grown in Zones 3 to 9.

Q&A

I have a spirea bush that is out of control. Should I trim it? If so, when would be the best time?

Annette Henry
MCKEESPORT, PENNSYLVANIA

Melinda: Prune spring-flowering spireas right after they bloom if you need to control their size but want to enjoy the blossoms. For summer-blooming spireas, take in their chestnut-brown stems and dried seed heads during the cold season and then cut them back in late winter or early spring before growth begins. Cut the plant back halfway and remove half of those stems to the ground.

While looking for trilliums, I discovered this unusual bloom among the normal ones. What caused this? Can I expect it to happen again?

Rebecca Landwehr MATTOON, WISCONSIN

Melinda: What a wonderful surprise! There have been reports from a few lucky hikers who have found these in the wild. They are also for sale at a few specialty nurseries. It's not uncommon for plants to mutate or morph in response to the environment or pest damage or simply over time. Sometimes the change is permanent and other times it is not. Note the location and visit next year to see if this special trillium returns.

DID YOU KNOW?
Trilliums typically have three petals on top of three sepals and bloom in early spring.

American wisteria

My wisteria has beautiful full foliage, but no blooms. In early summer, small round berries appear. What is wrong?

Bev Lutkenhaus CALMAR, IOWA

Melinda: Those little berries are likely flower buds. Late spring frosts, fluctuating temperatures and overly dry soil can prevent buds from opening or cause them to drop off the plant completely. Chances are you're growing a type of Asian wisteria—Chinese or Japanese. Some of these varieties can take more than 15 years before they bloom. Midwest gardeners usually have better success growing American wisteria (*Wisteria frutescens*). It may be a bit less spectacular than the Asian wisterias because the flowers appear with the leaves, but it is a more reliable bloomer.

My lilac bushes have never bloomed. They get some direct sun, but some shade. The soil is acidic because of pine and oak trees. Is this the problem?

Joanne Eastman LOVELL, MAINE

Melinda: Evergreen needles and oak leaves have little to no impact on soil acidity. Plus, acidic soil would cause leaf discoloration and stunted growth, not merely a lack of flowers. The shade from these trees may be the culprit. Lilacs flower best with at least six hours of direct sunlight. Too much high-nitrogen fertilizer and improper pruning can also result in a lack of flowers. Go easy on the fertilizing, and prune only if needed right after the lilacs should have bloomed. These plants develop their flower buds in the summer, and the buds then open the following spring.

I have six David Austin English roses in my yard. A couple of them have blooms that droop over and hang almost upside down. What causes this?

Gayle Romines
GREENBACKVILLE, VIRGINIA

Melinda: Large rose blossoms, common on many David Austin roses, often nod or droop. This does vary with varieties. As the plant matures and stems become thicker, the plant provides better support for the blossoms and the drooping is less noticeable. Prune the plants by no more than half in the winter, and fertilize twice a year with a low-nitrogen, organically based fertilizer. These steps will promote sturdy growth without interfering with flowering.

BACKYARD TIP
David Austin roses are known for being beautiful, yet easy to maintain.

Ten years ago I planted a smoke tree in full sun in my yard. The "poofs" of smoke begin to form in spring, but dry up. What should I do?

Betty Shafer MUSKEGON, MICHIGAN

Melinda: The smoky poofs are the hairy flower stems that become apparent once the less showy blooms drop. They change color throughout the summer until they turn that smoky pink that so many gardeners appreciate. Overly dry soil or late spring frosts can cause flowers, stem and all, to drop off the plant. Avoid high-nitrogen fertilizers that can interfere with flowering and be sure to prune only as needed. Expect to see a decline in flowering the following year, since these plants flower on 2- or 3-year-old wood.

BACKYARD TIP
All trees, thin- or thick-barked, can be damaged by a lawn mower or weed whacker.

What is this plant? I saw it on someone's porch.

Holly Harnly MYERSTOWN, PENNSYLVANIA

Melinda: The fuzzy flowers inspired common names like chenille plant and red-hot cat's tail. Botanically known as *Acalypha hispida*, this popular houseplant is often moved outdoors for summer in full to partial shade. Keep it in bloom by removing flowers as they fade. When temperatures cool in fall, move it back indoors to a warm, sunny window. Gardeners in Zones 10 and 11 can grow chenille plants outdoors year-round, and those plants can reach 10 feet tall and 8 feet wide.

About five years ago, I replaced overgrown lawn with a mixture of natives and herbs for birds and butterflies. But now, purple loosestrife has appeared along my property line. Is there any way to get rid of it, or am I doomed to a loosestrife takeover?

Marge Berger ATHENS, WISCONSIN

Melinda: Thanks for doing your part to keep invasive plants, like purple loosestrife, out of the ecosystem. Removing these invaders as soon as you find them, before they set seed, is the best way to control small populations. Plants in your neighborhood may be providing the seeds that are infesting your plantings. Work with neighbors to rid your area of this pest. Some severely infested communities have enlisted the help of galerucella beetles, which eat purple loosestrife leaves and prevent the plant from flowering. For information, contact the Wisconsin Department of Natural Resources. Officials work with schools and citizen groups to raise, release and monitor the beetles. Those battling purple loosestrife in other states can contact their local municipality, university extension office or Department of Natural Resources.

Purple loosestrife

Coming Up Roses

Tips for a garden that'll leave you blushing with pride. **By Kirsten Sweet**

CHOOSE

Bare-root rose plants perform best if you plant in spring while dormant, but container roses can be put in the ground anytime. If you're looking for ease, many new varieties are hardier and more disease-resistant, and deliver attractive plants that bloom all summer. New rose varieties take up less space. They're bred for gardeners with smaller yards and less time.

PLANT

Dig a wide hole the same depth as the roots, leaving a cone of soil in the middle, in a spot that receives 6 to 8 hours of full sun each day. To avoid disturbing the roots of container plants, cut away the pot rather than pulling out the plant. Many roses are grafted. The bud graft is easy to spot—it's the swollen knob with branches sprouting from it. In warm areas, like the South, plant the bud graft above ground level. In colder climates, where temperatures dip below freezing, plant it 1 to 2 inches below the soil surface.

TEND

A newly planted rose is going to be thirsty. Create a trough of soil around the plant, check daily and water as needed. Once established, only about an inch of water per week is needed. Watering on the ground, not from above, reduces the risk of disease. Add mulch, like bark, pine needles or shredded leaves, to conserve moisture and reduce weeding.

TRIM

To keep roses blooming throughout the growing season, remove spent flowers, a technique called deadheading. This transfers the plant's energy into creating even more blooms. Trim down to the first or second five-leaflet leaf.

SEVEN TYPES OF ROSES

Polyantha: introduced before 1867

Hybrid tea: showy, most popular

Floribunda: shrubby with bloom clusters

Grandiflora: tall, ideal for cut flowers

Miniature: only 6 to 18 inches

Shrub: large and full; some are fragrant

Climbing: use with trellises, arbors and walls

A shrub rose called Grace from David Austin Roses

Sunflower
Finalist in our
Backyard Photo Contest
Photo by Monica Brill

Spider flower
Photo by Katina Smith

Poppy
Finalist in our
Backyard Photo Contest
Photo by Steve Villagomez

Daylily
Finalist in our
Backyard Photo Contest
Photo by Brian Fox

Gazania
Finalist in our
Backyard Photo Contest
Photo by Lee Hooker

CHAPTER 6

Travel

Discover terrific places to go birding each season. Learn about the birds of the North Woods, the birdiest hot spots on the Appalachian Trail and where to see rare species in the U.S. Plus, explore historical gardens!

SEAN PAVONE/ISTOCK

follow that

BIRD!

The best part about birding is that you can do it anytime, anywhere, including in your own backyard. But if you're up for traveling this year, get out there and explore the world of birds, no matter the season. Check out these birding hot spots from coast to coast.
By Ken Keffer

Vermilion flycatchers can be spotted at Saguaro National Park in Arizona, where there is no shortage of desert scrub habitat.

Winter Hot Spots

When it comes to winter birding, you have two options: Embrace the cold weather or avoid it entirely. For a full dose of winter birding in crisp temperatures, Sax-Zim Bog, northwest of Duluth, Minnesota, is the place to be. You might not tally more than 50 species during your visit, but the unique birds you will find, including snowy owls, great gray owls and northern hawk owls, will more than make up for it.

If you'd rather migrate south like the birds, try Florida or the Desert Southwest. Birding locations in these areas are almost as abundant as the birds themselves. Florida's Everglades National Park, J.N. "Ding" Darling National Wildlife Refuge and the first National Wildlife Refuge, Pelican Island, are ideal destinations for waterbirds such as the roseate spoonbill and the sanderling.

In the Southwest, some of my favorite places for winter birding are Saguaro National Park in Arizona, home to vermilion flycatchers, and the Bosque del Apache National Wildlife Refuge in New Mexico.

Great egrets wade in and around the waters of Everglades National Park, standing about 3 feet tall.

White pelicans spend winters at J.N. "Ding" Darling National Wildlife Refuge.

Black-and-white warblers (and about 35 other warbler species) wow northwest Ohio visitors each spring.

Florida's Everglades National Park is an ideal destination for waterbirds such as the roseate spoonbill, anhinga and great egret.

Really get in the spirit of winter birding with the Christmas Bird Count, the longest-running citizen science project in the world. This partnership among the National Audubon Society, Bird Studies Canada and the Cornell Lab of Ornithology began in 1900. Now there are nearly 2,500 count circles each winter.

Spring Hot Spots

Whatever you do, don't step outside in spring without binoculars. Spring is the best season for migration, and one of the earliest migrations is the most spectacular. In March, more than 500,000 sandhill cranes, along with ducks and geese, congregate along the Platte River in central Nebraska. It might not feel like spring behind the

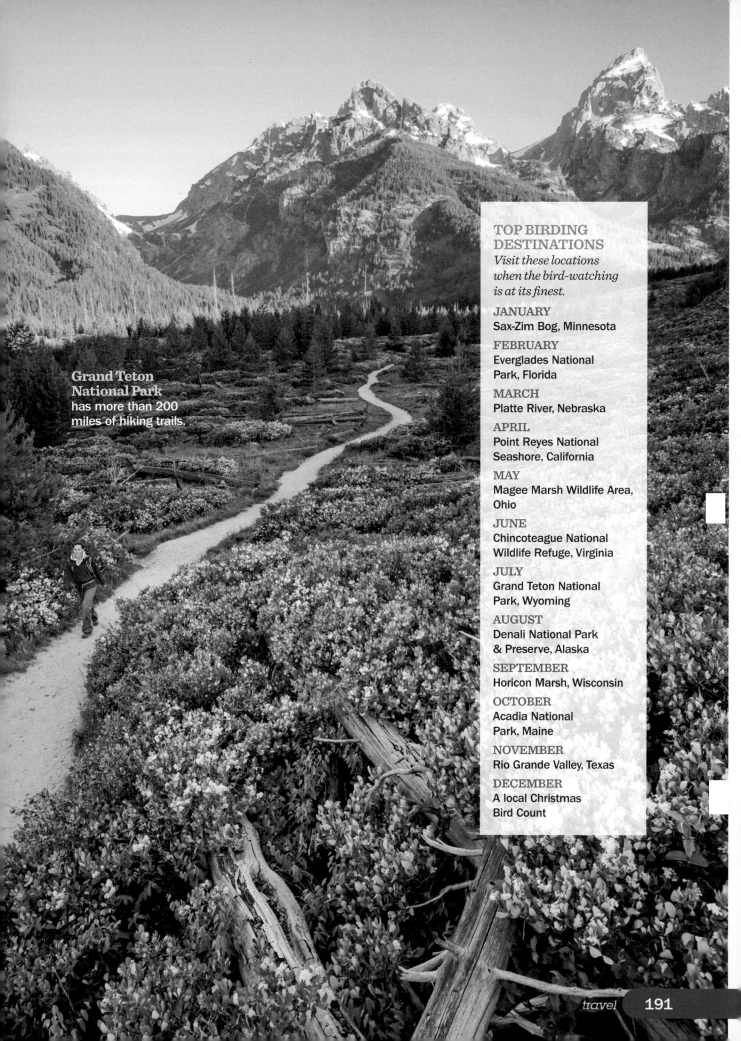

Grand Teton National Park has more than 200 miles of hiking trails.

TOP BIRDING DESTINATIONS

Visit these locations when the bird-watching is at its finest.

JANUARY
Sax-Zim Bog, Minnesota

FEBRUARY
Everglades National Park, Florida

MARCH
Platte River, Nebraska

APRIL
Point Reyes National Seashore, California

MAY
Magee Marsh Wildlife Area, Ohio

JUNE
Chincoteague National Wildlife Refuge, Virginia

JULY
Grand Teton National Park, Wyoming

AUGUST
Denali National Park & Preserve, Alaska

SEPTEMBER
Horicon Marsh, Wisconsin

OCTOBER
Acadia National Park, Maine

NOVEMBER
Rio Grande Valley, Texas

DECEMBER
A local Christmas Bird Count

Red-naped sapsuckers can be seen during visits to the Rocky Mountains.

Piping plovers often follow the East Coast shoreline on their spring and fall migrations.

bird blind, though; temperatures often dip below freezing, so bundle up for this incredible experience.

Watching a concentration of spring migrants, you'll feel as if you've won the birding jackpot. Dozens of songbird species refuel along the coast in Texas, Louisiana, Alabama and Mississippi after making the nonstop flight over the Gulf of Mexico. Northwest Ohio has birds galore, especially warblers, which cluster on the southern shore of Lake Erie before moving north.

Even if you can't go far in spring, you can search for the migrating birds that come your way. Hit your local park; scope out your neighborhood. If you're paying attention, you'll see birds on the move. I've nearly been late for work because I couldn't tear myself away from the constant movement of migratory birds flitting through the trees in my own backyard. One spring, I spotted magnolia, black-and-white, Canada and yellow-rumped warblers in a single flock.

Summer Hot Spots

A trip to a classic vacation destination can easily turn into a unique bird-watching opportunity. The western mountain national parks, including Glacier in Montana, Yellowstone and Grand Teton in Wyoming, and Rocky Mountain in Colorado, are great places to see high-elevation species. Look for red-naped sapsuckers and black-backed and three-toed woodpeckers while you hike through the forests. Keep an eye out along mountain stream rapids in case an American dipper is bobbling along with you.

Prefer the coasts? National wildlife refuges dot the Pacific and Atlantic shorelines like pearls on a necklace. You can explore urban nature habitats, including San Diego Bay National Wildlife Refuge in California and Chincoteague National Wildlife Refuge in Virginia, by bicycle.

Autumn Hot Spots

The Midwest is the ideal region for fall bird-watching. Quivira National Wildlife Refuge and Cheyenne Bottoms Wildlife Area in central Kansas are legendary stopover locations for shorebirds, ducks and geese, which gather by the thousands. These areas also see the occasional whooping crane. And don't forget the Mississippi River, which is like an interstate highway for birds in fall.

To see birds against a vibrant backdrop of fall color, head to Acadia National Park in Maine or the White Mountains of New Hampshire. Or follow migrants down the Atlantic Coast to Cape May in New Jersey and Kiptopeke State Park in Virginia. An array of migrants, from piping plovers to peregrine falcons, move south along the East Coast all autumn.

Whether you tally the birds visiting your feeder or explore the back roads of your bird count circle, make your local Christmas Bird Count a yearly tradition. One of my favorite memories was spotting a pine grosbeak while snowshoeing in Wyoming for a Christmas Bird Count. What a great end to a year of bird-watching!

Bring On Spring Birds

Check out these special, must-see hot spots.

Washington
1

Wyoming
Ontario

Nevada
2

3

4
Ohio
5

Male sooty grouse

Alpine meadow in the Snowy Range

American bittern

❶ OLYMPIC NATIONAL PARK, PORT ANGELES, WASHINGTON
Located on Washington's Olympic Peninsula, this park offers diverse habitats—glacier-capped mountains, wild Pacific coast, rivers and lakes, and rain forest. In the spring, rainfall is lighter and birds appear in the towering old-growth forests and along the rugged coastline. Look for varied thrush, sooty grouse and Pacific wren in the woods, and rhinoceros auklet, black oystercatcher and the threatened marbled murrelet at the coast.

❷ STILLWATER NATIONAL WILDLIFE REFUGE, NEVADA
This refuge protects a portion of the Lahontan Valley Wetlands, a designated Site of Hemispheric Importance to migrant shorebirds. Flashy species like black-necked stilt, American avocet and Arctic-breeding long-billed dowitcher are frequent visitors.

❸ SNOWY RANGE, MEDICINE BOW NATIONAL FOREST, WYOMING
The Rockies are the setting for this little range and extensive forest, which provide a chance to see mountain species in the spring. The brown-capped rosy-finch, Clark's nutcracker and American pipit are favorites, but venture out at night and you may hear the hooting of a rare boreal owl!

❹ POINT PELEE NATIONAL PARK, LEAMINGTON, ONTARIO
Few places can compare to the songbird migration at this Canadian national park known as the Warbler Capital of Canada, just an hour from the Michigan border. Birds making the flight across the Great Lakes often rest in the park's forest and wetlands. Keep your eyes peeled for Canada and Blackburnian warblers.

❺ OTTAWA NATIONAL WILDLIFE REFUGE, OAK HARBOR, OHIO
Diverse habitats at this refuge include wetland, grassland and forest, where you might be lucky enough to spot an American bittern or yellow-headed blackbird. Visit the area during the Biggest Week in American Birding festival, the ultimate celebration of warblers and other spring migrants.

Yellow warblers are one of many migrant species that pass through Point Pelee National Park.

Consider the Birds!

Spring is a great time to watch birds, but remember that our feathered friends are preparing to breed or are in the midst of a long migration. Be respectful of them, and don't come too close or do anything that might disturb their normal activities.

Great gray owls live year-round in the boreal forest and western mountains of the U.S.

meet the BOR

An astonishing number of species spend their days in

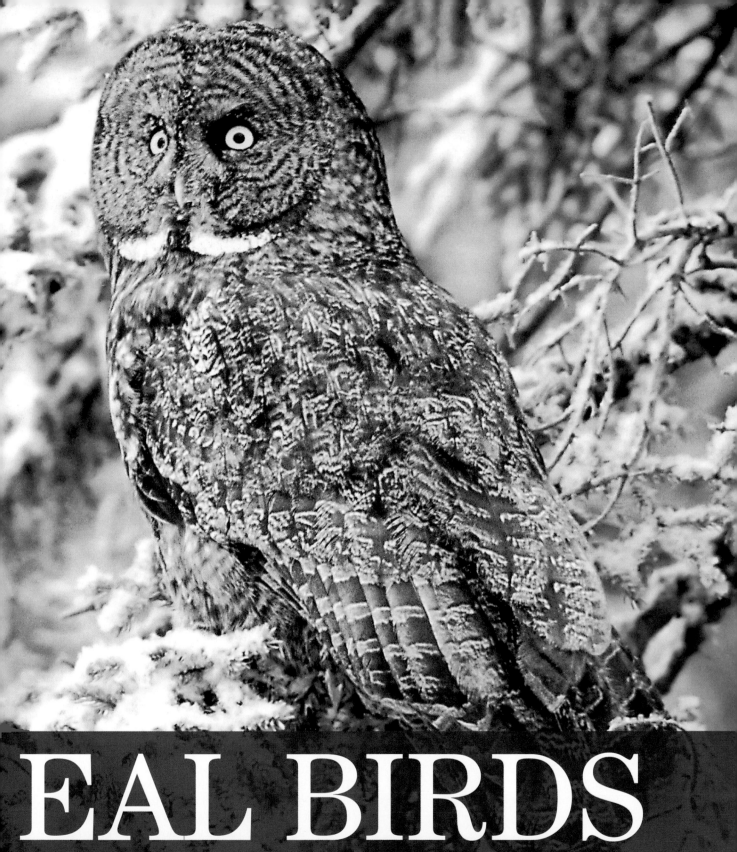

EAL BIRDS

the harsh habitat of the North Woods. **By David Shaw**

It's cold, buried in snow for much of the year and infested with mosquitoes and biting flies for the rest of the year. Seems like an inhospitable place, doesn't it? Not to everyone. The North Woods, as the boreal forest is also called, is one of the largest ecosystems on earth. It stretches around the northern quarter of the planet, across three continents. In North America, the habitat is mostly in Canada and Alaska, though small portions reach down into the upper Midwest and Northeast. It's a rough, wild and dark place, but for a staggering number of birds, that huge swath of woods is something else: home.

Northern goshawks maneuver through dense forest to search for food.

LONG, CHILLY DAYS

On a frigid January day, when the sun is above the horizon for just a few hours, the boreal forest can seem lifeless. Then, suddenly, it isn't. Flocks of boreal and black-capped chickadees materialize, their calls bouncing back and forth as they move through the trees. A downy or hairy woodpecker may appear with the group, tapping dead branches as it probes for hibernating insect larvae. Above, a raven passes, croaking. Gliding through the woods like a ghost, a hulking northern goshawk spooks a ruffed or spruce grouse from its resting place on a low branch.

The few resident species use a variety of adaptations to survive the long winter. Chickadees cache food during

Unlike many birds, ruffed grouse are able to digest the buds and twigs of aspen and birch trees, a food source that helps them survive extreme winters.

summer, and use their remarkable memory to recover it when they need it most. The grouse move into the trees to dine on spruce tips, or forage through the brambles looking for frozen berries left over from autumn. Flocks of redpolls, northern finches, take advantage of many pairs of eyes to search for rich foraging areas. Redpolls store seeds in a small pouch in their esophagus, which they draw on during the long, bitterly cold nights.

ERUPTING WITH ACTIVITY

By March and April, the sun is rising far above the horizon. The first spring migrants arrive as the snow begins to melt. Dark-eyed juncos are almost always the first to come back, but within days, more species arrive: American robins, ruby-crowned kinglets, yellow-rumped warblers and white-crowned and fox sparrows. The silence of winter disappears along with the snow by May, when about 150 bird species fill the boreal forest with song.

Summers are short in the north; both the migrant and resident birds make the most of the long days. They establish territories, pair up, build nests, lay eggs and raise their young in less time than do birds who breed farther south. Some species, like the alder flycatcher, spend an average of fewer than 50 days on their breeding grounds. In Alaska, this diminutive gray-green bird arrives in early June and is often gone before the end of July. Other species are also in a rush, and with little time to nest again if something goes wrong, they are under pressure to succeed.

By August, the area is teeming with newly fledged songbirds, and the ponds are dotted with broods of ducklings. Mixed-species flocks form and move through the forest, searching for food while keeping a wary eye out for predators. Orange-crowned, yellow, blackpoll and yellow-rumped warblers mix with juncos and white-crowned, Lincoln's and American tree sparrows as they flit through the trees. The breeding season has passed; now the young birds are practicing their songs like kids

▶▶ Pine grosbeaks occasionally wander in small flocks from their year-round home into the northern U.S. to feed on berries and maple buds.

Birds like the greater white-fronted goose use the wetlands of the boreal forest during spring and fall migrations to and from their Arctic breeding grounds.

Trumpeter swans, shown here at their British Columbia wintering grounds, weigh more than any other North American waterfowl.

Yukon-Charley Rivers
National Preserve, Alaska

Experience the Boreal Forest

The northern forest is huge and wild, but these areas are accessible to bird-watchers.

Boundary Waters Canoe Area Wilderness, Superior National Forest, Minnesota. Part of the southern reach of the boreal forest extends into northern Minnesota. Huge lakes, winding rivers, meadows and woods are habitat for 163 nesting bird species, including 24 warblers.

Terra Nova National Park, Newfoundland, Canada. Canada's easternmost national park combines ancient boreal forest with a stunning coastline, forming a perfect habitat for birds. The park is a globally recognized Important Bird Area.

Yukon-Charley Rivers National Preserve, Alaska. Encompassing 3,946 square miles of mountains, rivers, forest and lakes, this area is not easy to get to, but it's worth the effort. Millions of songbirds, waterfowl and shorebirds breed and migrate through the preserve each year.

learning new musical instruments. The resulting notes are mixed-up and off-key and never fail to bring a smile to the listener.

A NEW CYCLE BEGINS

In October, the last of the trumpeter and tundra swans migrate. In white V's they pass over the mountains and forests on their way to their southern wintering grounds. The other migrants are gone, and the few resident species are left alone as snow settles in once more.

The boreal forest is rugged, wild and often punishing. Unlike other landscapes, such as the mountains or coasts, the boreal forest takes effort to fully appreciate. The birds are easy to love, though.

In winter, most of the birds of the North Woods scatter like a cloud of confetti. You'll find them from the southern tip of South America to the American Great Plains, from the swamps of the Southeast to the coastal estuaries of the West.

Spend more than a few minutes watching a bird feeder or glassing ducks at the local pond or birding along a coast, and odds are excellent that a good portion of the birds you see will have hatched or migrated through the boreal forest. It's a nursery for an estimated 3 billion birds. Without them, not only the north, but the entire continent would be sadly bereft. The boreal forest is essential because the birds that depend on it are a part of all of our lives.

Experience the Appalachian

Grab some binoculars and hike your way to the trail's birdiest spots. **By Ken Keffer**

Mount Katahdin, Maine

Springer Mountain, Georgia

Known as the country's most famous footpath, the 2,190-mile Appalachian Trail stretches from Georgia to Maine, with no shortage of birds along the way. Add a few of these stops to your bucket list.

❶ AMICALOLA FALLS STATE PARK

Challenge yourself to climb the 600 steps to the top of Georgia's Amicalola Falls. Once you catch your breath and take in the picture-perfect view, set off on an 8-mile hike to Springer Mountain, the southernmost point of the trail. Keep a field guide handy because southern favorites, like hooded, yellow-throated and Kentucky warblers, are spotted here.

❷ GREAT SMOKY MOUNTAINS NATIONAL PARK

Slow down along this stretch and hear red-eyed vireos belt out their songs. Keep your eyes and ears open for blue-headed, yellow-throated and white-eyed vireos, too. Bird diversity explodes here in Tennessee and North Carolina. Southern species spend time in lower elevations, and northern

Look and listen for blue-headed vireos (inset) at Great Smoky Mountains National Park.

regulars reside in the higher forests. The 8-mile round-trip hike to Charlies Bunion, a stone outcrop, is classic Appalachian Trail terrain, with steep inclines and dense forests, plus some stunning glimpses of mountains and valleys.

❸ SHENANDOAH NATIONAL PARK

Escape to this Virginia hot spot, where nearly 200 bird species have been seen (roughly half of them breed here). Hikers see wild

turkeys foraging along the forest floor and barred owls in trees above. Shenandoah includes 101 miles of the Appalachian Trail and 400 miles of additional paths. For a quick way to get a taste of the woods, try the Frazier Discovery Trail; it's only about a mile long.

❹ DELAWARE WATER GAP NATIONAL RECREATION AREA

Visit during migration and look for large flocks of broad-winged hawks soaring

high above Kittatinny Ridge, an integral part of the Atlantic Flyway. Winter brings concentrations of bald eagles and an occasional golden eagle to the park, which stretches along both sides of the Pennsylvania-New Jersey border. Hike any of the 27 miles of the trail, or hop on the Delaware River to bird-watch by canoe or by kayak.

Bald eagle

TRAIL TRIVIA

More than 150 million people live within a day's drive of the Appalachian Trail, so the entire path plays a huge role in connecting people to nature.

Rare Bird Hot Spots

Explore the corners of the U.S. to find the unusual species on your bucket list.

U.S. Fish and Wildlife Service vessel with crested auklets

Sonny Bono Salton Sea National Wildlife Refuge

Country road at Hartwick Pines State Park

❶ ALASKA MARITIME NATIONAL WILDLIFE REFUGE, ALASKA

Encompassing a scattering of islands and mainland habitat across western Alaska, this refuge is home for a staggering 40 million seabirds. Species that nest only in the far north—like horned puffins, red-legged kittiwakes, and least, crested and parakeet auklets—are in abundance in spring and summer.

❷ SONNY BONO SALTON SEA NATIONAL WILDLIFE REFUGE, CALIFORNIA

Famous for the huge number of shorebirds and waterfowl that winter and migrate through the refuge, Salton Sea is also a magnet for vagrants and rarities. Keep your eyes open for rarely seen birds such as ruffs, blue-footed boobies and yellow-footed gulls.

❸ BENTSEN-RIO GRANDE VALLEY STATE PARK, TEXAS

A little pocket of the tropics at the southern tip of Texas, the park is the only place this side of the border where you can see species like green jays, chachalacas, great kiskadees, least grebes, Altamira orioles, white-tipped doves and ringed kingfishers.

❹ HARTWICK PINES STATE PARK, MICHIGAN

The main attraction here is the endangered Kirtland's warbler, which survives thanks to the careful management of jack pine forests. If you want to see this rare bird for yourself, you can join a free guided tour with the Michigan Audubon Society. Tours run from mid-May to early July. Groups of five or more need to make a reservation.

❺ ACADIA NATIONAL PARK, MAINE

The first national park in the East, Acadia is a diverse landscape of rugged coast, forests and mountains—and 338 bird species have been recorded in the park. More than 20 species of warblers alone can be found here, and the rock coastlines are home to uncommon seabirds like the Atlantic puffin.

Acadia National Park

What Makes a Bird Rare?

Though some species, like the endangered Kirtland's warbler, are threatened because of human impact, a few that we consider rare are vagrant birds that don't normally appear in North America. Others, like the seabirds in Alaska, number in the millions but occur only up north.

Seeds of History

Go back in time and step into four gardens rooted in America's past. **By David Shaw**

Alcatraz Island

From a Founding Father's orchard to a former prison garden, our nation's history crops up in the unlikeliest of places. Visit these plots from the past and get a glimpse of what life was like back then—no time machine required.

Vegetable gardens at Monticello

❶ MONTICELLO, CHARLOTTESVILLE, VIRGINIA

Imagined, designed and built by Thomas Jefferson, Monticello reflects the Founding Father's vision to this day. The grounds surrounding his grand home are filled with flower, vegetable and fruit gardens, each with hundreds of heirloom varieties dating to the 1700s. Stroll along paths that wind through shady groves to truly appreciate why Jefferson is known as "the father of American forestry."
monticello.org

❷ GRAND PORTAGE NATIONAL MONUMENT, GRAND PORTAGE, MINNESOTA

The North West Co. operated a trading post at Grand Portage, Minnesota, from 1778 to 1803 that included extensive gardens. The National Park Service now maintains two, a traders' kitchen garden and a Native American one, growing vegetable varieties that date back 200 years. Visitors learn how the seed trade carried fruits and veggies westward and how the three sisters planting

Grand Portage

style of the Ojibwe people integrated corn, beans and squash to keep soil at maximum productivity.
nps.gov/grpo

❸ GLEN LEVEN FARM, NASHVILLE, TENNESSEE

Thomas Thompson founded this 65-acre farm just outside Nashville as part of a Revolutionary War land grant in 1790. Six generations later, in 2006, a descendant bequeathed it to the Land Trust for Tennessee. The working farm has an arboretum with trees planted in the late 1800s, as well as extensive varieties of heirloom daffodils. Although the farm isn't regularly open to the public, it offers organized tours and workshops.
landtrusttn.org

❹ ALCATRAZ ISLAND, SAN FRANCISCO, CALIFORNIA

A military prison seems an odd place for a garden, and originally even the thin soil was unwelcoming. After Alcatraz opened in 1861, the military hauled in soil from Angel Island and the Presidio, and began planting in 1865. The California Spring Blossom and Wildflower Association worked with inmates in the 1920s to cover the island with flowers. The tradition continued after Alcatraz became a federal prison. It closed in 1963, but the hard work of the past still grows, thanks to the National Park Service and nonprofit collaborators.
alcatrazgardens.org

PLANT THE PAST Heirlooms add historical flavor to your garden. Research what was grown in your region and then see what you can re-create with commercially available heirloom seeds to spice up your space while helping to protect native plants.

homegrown Harvest

Grow delicious heirloom veggies, the perfect hot peppers, savory herbs and more! Cultivate ingredients for making homemade tea and beer. The expert advice here will turn your thumb green in no time, and you'll reap the benefits.

GAP PHOTOS

REAP THE MANY BENEFITS OF TIMELESS,

Challenging climates have nothing on heirlooms. These classic open-pollinated plants not only connect us to the long history of gardening because of their age, but over time, they've adapted to local conditions, making them solid choices for your backyard. Gardeners should select heirloom varieties from their region or an area with similar conditions in order to get the most out of the plants.

HEIRLOOM BASICS

Tor Janson, collection curator for the nonprofit Seed Savers Exchange (*seedsavers.org*), compares these plants to family keepsakes because the seeds are passed down through generations. Heirlooms are open-pollinated, which means they are pollinated naturally by insects, birds, humans and the wind. They also self- and cross-pollinate.

The seeds usually stay true to type over time. This makes their behavior in the garden easier to predict than that of hybrids, which are the result of cross-breeding of two varieties. Hybrids rarely stay true in successive generations.

"Generally, heirloom varieties that have been grown over generations in a particular area tend to work well there," Janson says.

# of Heirlooms

REGION-SPECIFIC VEGGIES. By Heather Lamb

THE HOT AND HUMID SOUTHEAST

Long growing seasons with high heat and humidity are hard on a lot of vegetables. "Many crops can't cope," says Randel Agrella, seed production manager for Baker Creek Heirloom Seeds (*rareseeds.com*). Selecting the right plants is one way to deal with the heat, but Agrella also suggests gardening from fall to spring instead of during the summer.

Switching the growing season will have the most impact on tomatoes, a crop affected by sustained high temperatures. Agrella recommends eastern European tomato varieties, which develop full flavor in cool weather, for late-summer planting. For spring planting, try southern European types that ripen in the heat.

Ira Wallace of Southern Exposure Seed Exchange (*southernexposure.com*), an heirloom resource for Southern gardeners, says smaller tomato varieties tend to be less demanding and better withstand high heat. Wallace particularly likes Cherokee Purple tomatoes, which the company introduced to the seed-buying market.

Beyond tomatoes, there's a wealth of veggies that thrive in the heat and humidity of the Southeast, including okra, watermelon, pole beans, collards and bell peppers.

Emilee Gettle (left) and her husband, Jere, own Baker Creek Heirloom Seeds. Even their seed packets (right) have an old-fashioned feel.

Buying Heirloom Seeds

Many seed companies and seed banks specialize in heirloom and open-pollinated seeds. When buying, look for sources that support the mission of seed saving or those that have signed the Safe Seed Pledge from the Council for Responsible Genetics.

THE COOL MIDWEST AND NORTHWEST

Where the summers are short and relatively cool, such as in the Northwest and upper Midwest, look for varieties of tomatoes, bell peppers, eggplant and watermelon that mature quickly.

Cool stretches interspersed among the hot days can affect growth. "Not all days are created equal," Agrella says. "Ninety days to maturity means 90 fairly ideal days." Instead, he suggests selecting varieties labeled as 80 days to maturity.

Timing and starting seeds indoors are important in short-season areas. Varieties from the Pacific Northwest and eastern Europe generally also work well in the Northeast and upper Midwest, as do local heirlooms, Agrella says.

THE DRY AND ARID SOUTHWEST

Many vegetables are difficult to grow in the hot and dry Southwest. "Most common crops are going to be a challenge," Agrella says. In these regions, intercropping, or companion planting, makes better use of the land and often boosts productivity, according to Gary Paul Nabhan in his book *Growing Food in a Hotter, Drier Land.* So, a vine such as pole bean or melon climbs up a tall crop like corn or sorghum.

PART OF THE PAST

Gardening with heirlooms isn't just about practicality. Planting seeds that have been carefully passed from one generation to the next fosters an emotional connection. "I like the sense that I'm connected to this thing that goes back to the beginning of agriculture," Agrella says. "It's the feeling of being part of something."

And that's the real magic.

Illini Star tomato plants produce early crops of round, red fruit.

47

VEGGIE PICKS BY CLIMATE

HOT AND HUMID

Bell peppers: Ashe County Pimiento, Doe Hill Golden Bell

Collards: Morris Heading

Okra: Cajun Jewel

Peanuts: Schronce's Deep Black

Pole beans: Louisiana Purple Pod, Selma Zesta

Tomatoes: *Late-summer planting:* Belarusian Heart, Black Prince, Brave General, Emerald Apple, Mushroom Basket, Stupice; *spring:* Comstock Sauce 'n' Slice, Costoluto Genovese, Cuor di Bue, Pantano Romanesco; *summer:* Bonny Best, Cherokee Purple, Eva Purple Ball, Placero

Watermelon: Moon & Stars, Strawberry

SHORT SEASON

Bell peppers: King of the North, Horizon, Oda

Bush beans: Contender, Roma II

Eggplant: Japanese Pickling, Japanese White Egg, Mitoyo

Tomatoes: Glacier, Sub-Arctic Plenty, Tess's Land Race Currant, and all late-summer varieties from the Hot and Humid list above

Watermelon: Blacktail Mountain, Cream of Saskatchewan, Sweet Dakota Rose

ARID

Beans: Rattlesnake (pole), Provider (bush)

Corn: Stowell's Evergreen, Yuman Yellow

Cucumber: Beit Alpha

Peppers: California Wonder, Chimayo

Tomatoes: Moonglow, Punta Banda, Yellow Pear

hot peppers

Bring the heat from your garden into the kitchen. BY LORI VANOVER

GARDEN TIP
Pepper plants have delicate branches that are easily harmed. Use scissors or a hand pruner to remove peppers from the plant.

Cayenne

TOP 10

1 HABANERO
2 ANAHEIM
3 THAI
4 SCOTCH BONNET
5 JALAPENO
6 TABASCO
7 PEPPERONCINI
8 CAYENNE
9 POBLANO
10 SERRANO

Peppers add a tantalizing jolt of flavor to your cooking. While it's getting easier to find a variety of fresh and dried peppers at the grocery store, it's much more fun and economical to grow your own. Start seeds indoors at least eight to 10 weeks before transplanting them into your garden, or look for starter plants at your garden center. By mid to late summer, you'll have ripe peppers ready to pick. And then the real fun begins—eating them!

▲ Habanero

If you're looking to fire up your food, throw in some habaneros. These small, wrinkled orange peppers are intensely hot with a slightly sweet flavor that is strongest when the pepper is used fresh in salsas or salads. Cooking will mellow out the heat somewhat. Habaneros require a warm environment to encourage the seeds to sprout, and the growing season is long.
Why we love it: It seems that exciting new varieties of habaneros are being developed all the time—and they're even hotter. I've especially enjoyed growing and eating the beautiful chocolate habanero.

▲ Anaheim

Even if this annual didn't grow to a height of 20 inches, it would still be a showstopper, thanks to its brilliant scarlet fruit. It thrives in containers or beds and is a fantastic performer through summer and fall.
Why we love it: Anaheim peppers are often used fresh to make salsa verde. The large size also makes them perfect for chiles relleno, the popular stuffed, battered and fried Mexican specialty.

◄ Thai

If you crave spicy noodle dishes from your favorite Asian restaurant, this is the pepper for you. As the name suggests, these peppers originated in Thailand, and they are hot, hot, hot. The slender, ½- to 1-inch peppers ripen from green to bright red.
Why we love it: The plant stays small, so it's a wise choice for ornamental use on your patio. Don't be afraid to slice up a few Thai peppers and toss them into your stir-fry or curry. They also keep well when preserved in oil or vinegar.

▲ Scotch bonnet

These fruity fireballs look similar to habaneros, but they are shorter and stouter, shaped like a little hat or bonnet. The plants are very slow-growing. If you want to have mature red peppers before frost in a northern zone, start the seeds indoors very early. I've grown Scotch bonnet plants in containers so I could bring them inside on chilly Wisconsin autumn nights.

Why we love it: I love spicy Caribbean cuisine, particularly jerk chicken. Along with allspice, these slightly sweet but blazing hot peppers are a key ingredient in every standout jerk recipe.

▲ Tabasco

The iconic smoky, vinegary hot sauce is made with Tabasco peppers grown on tiny Avery Island in southern Louisiana, about 140 miles west of New Orleans. Tabasco peppers require 80 to 100 days to reach maturity; they grow best in hot, humid weather. The prolific plants will be covered in small, shiny red peppers. If your growing season isn't long enough, try growing Tabasco peppers in a container in a sunny spot.

Why we love it: You might not be able to crack the famously secret Tabasco hot sauce recipe, but why not have fun trying?

▲ Jalapeno

Make space for several of these simple-to-grow plants in your garden. Jalapenos mature in 75 days, quicker than many other hot pepper varieties, so they're a good choice for northern gardeners. If you don't pick them right away, they'll turn red, but they taste fabulous either way! Dry and smoke jalapenos to make chipotle peppers.

Why we love it: The dark green pepper is perfect for stuffing, grilling, wrapping in bacon, pickling, or just eating raw on burgers and tacos.

▲ Pepperoncini

Want to pickle peppers or make giardiniera? Then leave room for these Italian favorites in your garden. Plants produce plenty of 5- to 6-inch light green peppers. Their pale color will change to bright red if you wait to pick them, but their flavor stays sweet and slightly spicy.

Why we love it: Pepperoncini are ideal for chopping up and throwing into a salad or piling onto a hot Italian beef sandwich.

8

▲ Cayenne

Even if you've never seen these long, skinny, curled peppers growing, you probably have some dried cayenne in your spice rack. These peppers start out green but aren't ready to harvest until they turn bright red. Because of their thin walls, they can be dried easily to cook with year-round or to use for decoration.

Why we love it: A healthy dash of cayenne pepper spices up chili, stew or barbecue.

9

▲ Poblano

These large, dark green, slightly sweet peppers are known by two names in Mexico: poblano when fresh and ancho when dried. They ripen to a deep, almost black color. Their heat is mild, and the bushy, easy-to-grow plants are heavy producers.

Why we love it: This pepper tastes wonderful when roasted and is the classic choice for chiles relleno. Ancho peppers are the main ingredient in Mexican mole sauces.

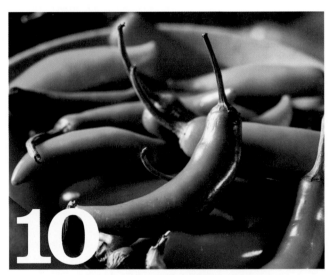

10

▲ Serrano

I'm glad I spotted this plant at my garden center last spring. I was looking for something slightly hotter than a jalapeno but not as intense as a habanero, and the serrano fit the bill. This high-yielding plant should produce plenty of finger-length, slender peppers all summer. I like them green, but some prefer them red.

Why we love it: Serranos are ideal when you want to add a fresh, flavorful punch to Mexican cuisine or perk up a pico de gallo.

tips for
productive peppers

- Start seeds indoors at least eight to 10 weeks before your last spring frost date.

- Pepper seeds need heat to sprout; around 80 degrees is optimal. If you don't have a heat mat, try placing them above your refrigerator.

- Some of the hottest peppers can take up to a month to germinate. Once they do sprout, place them under grow lights for about 16 hours per day.

- Peppers thrive in warm temperatures. Once plants have at least two true sets of leaves and the danger of frost has passed, begin to harden off by taking them outside for an hour or two in a sheltered location. Exposing them to too much sun will scald the leaves, but cold air can slow growth, so be cautious.

Grow Your Own Tea

Put the kettle on and brew a one-of-a-kind blend.

GROWING

True tea (white, black and green) comes from one plant species: *Camellia sinensis*, hardy in Zones 6 to 9. This plant isn't finicky (slightly acidic soil, a sunny location and plenty of water will keep it happy), but it grows slowly from seed. It can take three years to get a harvest and cuttings are challenging, so consider purchasing a plant instead. If you don't have the garden space for camellia, you may already have herbs in your garden, such as mint and lemongrass, that you can use for tisanes, or herbal teas.

HARVESTING

How you harvest camellia will determine the kind of tea you brew. Pluck pale gray leaf buds at the start of the growing season for white tea; when bright green leaves appear, pick those for green tea. Wilt plucked leaves for a day for black tea. Whether you pick buds or leaves, dry your harvest in an oven set to a low temperature (230 degrees or less).

If using herbs, research which part of the plant is used for making tea, such as the leaves of the mint plant, the buds and flowers of chamomile or the outer stalks of lemongrass. Freshly picked herbs can be brewed right away. You can also dry herbs to keep your cupboard stocked.

BREWING

Brewing tea all boils down to personal preference. Add about 1 tablespoon of tea blend per person to a kettle of just-boiled water you've taken off the heat. Let steep for five to 15 minutes, according to taste. Then, pour the brew through a tea strainer into each cup.

CUPS OF INSPIRATION

When it comes to herbal teas, the possibilities are almost endless. Here are a few to try:

Bee balm	Lemon verbena	Sage
Bergamot	Raspberry	Strawberry
Lavender	Rose hip	Yarrow

STEEPING TIPS

- Don't overfill the kettle. Judge the amount of water you need by how many cups you will serve right away.
- For the best-tasting tea, pour fresh water into the kettle for additional cups.
- Gently tear or crush herbal leaves, buds or roots to release essential oils and to boost flavor.
- Try a tea infuser or ball instead of a strainer for a simpler brewing process.

TRY THIS!
Plant your favorite herbs for tea, like basil and chamomile, in one container to make a miniature tea garden.

PLANT IT!
Grow hops in
well-draining soil.
The roots will rot
if there is any
standing water.

Brews & Blooms
Craft a truly unique beer by growing the ingredients yourself.

HOPS

From a perennial vine grown by rhizomes, hops give beer its bitterness. For the best results, grow several varieties of hops in a sunny spot with something to climb on—the aggressive vines can grow over 25 feet tall and weigh more than 20 pounds. Harvest in late summer and dry in a dark place with low humidity.

Plan ahead, because each plant produces up to 2 pounds of dried hops, and a barrel of beer usually requires 1 to 3 pounds of hops. Try Cascade, with citrus and grapefruit tones, or Golding, which has a mild, bitter flavor.

GRAINS

The essential component of beer, grains provide fermentable sugars used by yeast to make alcohol. Barley is the most popular choice for home brewers, but other grains, such as wheat, rice, corn, rye, oats and sorghum, can be used. These are easy to grow in your garden if you have the space, but note that using them for beer takes some time. The grains need to be malted—or steeped and germinated over several days—to extract the sugars needed for brewing. A home brew resource can provide information on malting.

For best results, plant at least two kinds of grains. You need about 25 to 40 pounds of malted barley for a barrel of beer.

FRUIT

Sweeten the brew with homegrown peaches, apples, pears, cherries, raspberries, blackberries or blueberries. For seasonal home brews, try pumpkin. Add the fresh fruit to the mash (recommended for pumpkin ales), or steep cut-up fruit in hot wort or add mashed fruit during the secondary fermentation (recommended for other fruit beers). Depending on the fruit you use and the desired flavor, you'll need 3 to 7 pounds of fruit per 5-gallon batch.

HERBS

Instead of or in addition to hops, consider using herbs to spice up a home brew. Typically, herbs are added during the boil or after the secondary fermentation (depending on the flavor profile you're after). Use about 1 ounce or less per 5-gallon batch.

HOME BREW GLOSSARY

- **Hops:** cone-shaped flowers that add flavor and bitterness to wort.
- **Malt:** grain that has been soaked, germinated and dried.
- **Mash:** crushed malt mixed with hot water.
- **Wort:** unfermented beer.

Enhancing herbs:
  Coriander: sweet, peppery, orange-like scent and flavor.
  Ginger: spicy flavors and aromas.
  Woodruff: cinnamon or vanilla flavors.
  Juniper: bittersweet flavors and aromas.
  Rose hips: sweetness to tartness, depending on taste.
  Yarrow: bitterness.

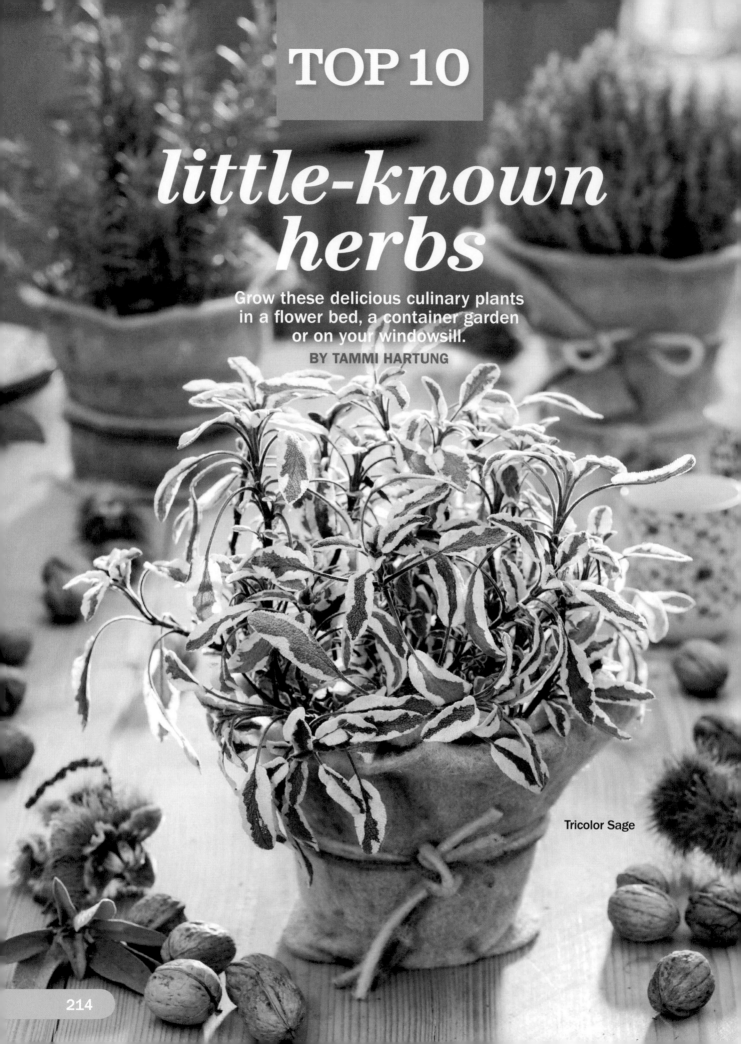

TOP 10
little-known herbs

Grow these delicious culinary plants
in a flower bed, a container garden
or on your windowsill.
BY TAMMI HARTUNG

Tricolor Sage

For those who like to cook and garden, growing herbs offers abundant choices. Handy in perennial or kitchen gardens, herbs can thrive in a range of light, soil and water conditions. Try some lesser-known varieties and you might find the perfect complement to your garden (and your cooking).

▲ Bronze fennel

FOENICULUM VULGARE 'RUBRUM', ZONES 7 TO 10

Fennel has a licorice taste that's a delight in some dishes. Most varieties are green, but this fennel has gorgeous bronze foliage that moves gracefully in the breeze. It's a tall perennial, reaching 3 to 4 feet, with yellow flower clusters that give way to delicious seeds. Fennel prefers full sun and moderate watering. Harvest seeds when they're ripe to prevent self-sowing.

Why we love it: The leafy parts are delicious when chopped fine into green or pasta salads, and especially with tomatoes. Seeds are awesome in Italian sauces and homemade sausage, and with baked vegetables like potatoes and squash.

▲ Garlic chives

ALLIUM TUBEROSUM, ZONES 4 TO 9

A lovely border herb, garlic chives are perennial and very hardy. They grow in sun or in shade and prefer moderate watering, but they tolerate drought or excessive moisture. They reach 10 to 24 inches, with clusters of white star-shaped flowers.

Why we love it: Garlic chives taste slightly stronger than ordinary chives but are not as pungent as garlic. Chop stalks into salsa or omelets or use them as a garnish on soups and noodle dishes. Sprinkle the flowers on a green salad for some zip without overwhelming it.

◄ Red-veined sorrel

RUMEX SANGUINEUS VAR. *SANGUINEUS,* ZONES 4 TO 9

This shade-loving sorrel has vivid green leaves with red veins and stems. The perennial reaches 18 to 24 inches and appreciates a bit of extra water, although it will tolerate moderate watering conditions.

Why we love it: The lemony flavor of red-veined sorrel is wonderful in salads and casseroles, or chopped into rice and served with salmon. Or make a wilted salad with equal amounts of spinach and red-veined sorrel, and top with bacon.

▲ Lime balm

MELISSA OFFICINALIS 'LIME', ZONES 5 TO 9

Like its cousin lemon balm, lime balm is perennial, and best in a partly shady location with moderate watering. It grows to about 24 inches, with delicate small white flowers. The foliage has the fragrance and taste of mild lime.

Why we love it: Add a generous tablespoon of chopped lime balm to fruit salad or mix it into cream cheese or butter to spread on bagels or pancakes.

▲ Fernleaf dill

ANETHUM GRAVEOLENS 'FERNLEAF', ZONES 6 TO 10

In most places, dill is a self-sowing annual. It grows nicely in sun or part shade and requires moderate watering. Fernleaf dill reaches 15 to 18 inches, making it ideal for containers or small gardens. This variety doesn't compete well with weeds, so keep the patch tidy.

Why we love it: Dill is one of the most versatile of culinary herbs. The leafy tops, sometimes called dill weed, brighten up deviled eggs and potato, green and pasta salads. A natural companion to potatoes, dill seed is good in potato-ham soup and scalloped potatoes. And, of course, dill is a must when making pickles.

▲ Dwarf winter savory

SATUREJA MONTANA 'NANA', ZONES 5 TO 9

Dwarf winter savory is a perennial with delicate white flowers and weeping branches. A small herb, growing 10 to 12 inches, this savory grows in sun or shade with moderate watering. Use leaves and flowers in cooking and harvest it throughout the growing season.

Why we love it: All varieties of winter savory go with lamb or beef; they're often used in hearty stews. Savory has a strong flavor, so use a light hand and adjust the amount to your taste. Try sprinkling it over potatoes fried in a bit of olive oil or butter.

▲ Tricolor sage

SALVIA OFFICINALIS 'TRICOLOR', ZONES 6 TO 9

This variegated green, pink and cream-colored culinary sage is a tender perennial that grows in sun or part shade, and prefers low watering. It has lovely purple-blue flowers and can get 15 to 18 inches tall.

Why we love it: All culinary sages complement chicken and turkey. Add sage to stuffing and grains, such as rice or quinoa. It has a strong flavor, so start conservatively and adjust to taste.

▲ Vietnamese coriander

POLYGONUM ODORATUM SYN. *PERSICARIA ODORATA,*
ZONES 10 AND 11

A tender perennial, this herb grows very nicely in a container or on a windowsill. It prefers indirect light and moderate to high watering. Grow Vietnamese coriander as ground cover or allow it to cascade over edges of containers or garden walls. In cold climates, treat it as an annual or bring it indoors for winter. Bright green with a dark marking on each leaf, Vietnamese coriander doesn't have flowers and stays under 10 inches.

Why we love it: It's a classic of Asian cuisine, often combined with fish sauce. Use in soup or noodle bowls or add to salads to get a full dose of its unique flavor.

▲ Hot and Spicy oregano

ORIGANUM VULGARE 'HOT AND SPICY', ZONES 5 TO 9

Hot and Spicy oregano is a cousin to Greek oregano. It grows to about 12 to 18 inches, with white flowers. Like most perennial oregano, it prefers sun and low to moderate watering.

Why we love it: Similar to Greek oregano, with a little more bite but not overly hot, this variety perks up pasta sauces and pizzas. It's also good with green beans and summer squash.

▲ Thyme

THYMUS SPECIES, ZONES 4 TO 9

Most thymes are perennial, but some variegated and golden varieties are annuals. They grow well in sun and part shade, with low water requirements. They cannot abide soggy roots or root crowns, so plant them in locations that drain well. Some lesser-known varieties include the fragrant Spicy Orange; Elfin, which grows in dense clumps; and Archer's Gold (above), with beautiful saffron foliage in winter. Upright thymes can reach 10 inches. Creeping thymes range from almost flat to 2 to 3 inches high, and typically spread as ground cover.

Why we love it: All varieties are edible, but some are easier than others to harvest. Add to meat, most vegetables or grains.

add more thyme to your garden

Thyme can grow between stepping-stones, over walls, in a rock garden or as a border plant. There are dozens of kinds, and all are fragrant and edible. Here are some thyme choices beyond the widely known culinary varieties.

- Caborn Wine & Roses
- Doone Valley Lemon
- English Wedgewood
- French Summer
- Lavender
- Lime (green or gold foliage)
- Magic Carpet
- Mother of Thyme
- Pink Chintz
- Porlock
- Reiter
- Shepherd's
- Silver Edge Lemon

GET STARTED
Grow an organic straw-bale garden with bales directly from a farm.

Straw-Bale Gardening
Try this smart and easy way to grow veggies.

Gardeners face challenges: poor soil, weeds, space issues and short growing seasons, to name a few. You can eliminate some of these challenges with straw bales, because the bales hold moisture and, as they decompose, they provide a rich medium for veggies.

"The biggest benefit of straw-bale gardening is that the bales heat up as they begin the 'conditioning' process, and thus allow earlier planting," says Joel Karsten, author of *Straw Bale Gardens Complete: Breakthrough Vegetable Gardening Method.* "The warm root zone means faster, early-season root

production and earlier-maturing vegetables."

Raised bales are easier to reach and work on for those with physical limitations. And they almost eliminate weeding, a benefit many straw-bale gardeners love most.

Follow these steps to garden with straw bales.

PICK A PRIME LOCATION.
Choose heavy, highly compressed straw (not hay!) bales, directly from a farm if possible. Find a location that gets six to eight hours of sunlight per day. Lay landscape fabric to keep weeds from growing, and arrange bales cut sides up, with strings on the sides.

CONDITION THE STRAW.
Two weeks before planting, start "cooking" the bales. Treat them with high-nitrogen fertilizer every other day and water heavily for about two weeks to accelerate decomposition of the straw inside the bale.

PLANT SEEDLINGS OR SEEDS.
Seedlings can be planted directly in the bales. Just make a hole with a trowel and add a little planting mix to cover the exposed roots. Seeds require a bed of potting soil to hold moisture on top of the bale until germination. If you wish, plant annual

flowers or herbs into the sides of the bales to make them more attractive.

PROTECT AND SUPPORT.
Position tall posts at the end of each row and run wire between them at 10-inch intervals from the top of the bale. When seeds sprout, drape a plastic tarp over the bottom wire to create a greenhouse for chilly nights. As the plants grow, the wires become a vertical trellis, supporting viny veggies.

HARVEST AND COMPOST.
When the season is over, the bales turn into usable, healthy compost for next year's gardens.

did you know?

DIG IN! Growing tips and fun facts about root vegetables.

3 Three things can cause spicy or sharp-tasting radishes: hot weather, dry soil or picking them too late.

1 Root vegetables need at least 1 inch of water per week to aid in good root development.

5 Have you ever seen a white carrot? These delicious veggies are available in five colors: orange, red, yellow, white and purple.

100 George Washington Carver developed more than 100 different products from sweet potatoes, including ink, synthetic silk, alcohol and paper.

6 It's a good idea to do a soil test before planting. An ideal pH range for root vegetables is between 6 and 6.8.

2 You've got two options when growing horseradish: Provide lots of room (it's an aggressive grower!) or set up boundaries to contain it.

10 It can take up to 10 months for ginger to mature, limiting the regions where it's grown.

4 There's a four-day festival dedicated to rutabagas. Visit the Annual Rutabaga Festival in Cumberland, Wisconsin.

butterflies, Bees & More

Help revive butterfly and bee populations in your neighborhood by growing plants specifically for them. Visit 14 butterfly hot spots that will set you aflutter, and get up close with some fascinating backyard hunters.

BUTTERFLY WORLD

ON A *monarch*

Team up with these ambassadors on a crusade to revive butterfly populations.

By Crystal Rennicke

MISSION

Be a monarch champion by planting native milkweeds in your backyard. The plants' leaves are monarch caterpillars' only source of food.

T HEIR INCREDIBLE LIFE CYCLE and awe-inspiring migration make monarchs one of the most beloved butterfly species in North America. In the past 20 years, however, populations have dropped dramatically, between 80 and 90 percent. For gardeners who love these winged guests, it's a heartbreaking statistic.

Three organizations in particular are fighting for monarchs. They tirelessly educate and motivate home gardeners to ensure that the impressive migration continues for future generations. Let these groups inspire you to be a butterfly hero today.

Monarch caterpillar on milkweed

Save Our Monarchs Foundation

Ward Johnson recalls his parents—both teachers and passionate gardeners—spending countless hours in their garden, planting host and nectar plants for butterflies. This deep-seated love of wildlife spurred Ward to establish Save Our Monarchs, a grassroots nonprofit that distributes milkweed seeds to the public.

Its motto is strong: "No milkweed, no monarchs." The small organization is dedicated to spreading the word about milkweed. "We don't want to just give away seeds," Ward says. "We want to educate people about why this is important and motivate them to plant."

Milkweed seeds are available via the foundation's website, *saveourmonarchs.org*. The group teams up with schools, garden clubs and smaller organizations

It takes 10 to 14 days for a monarch butterfly to go through the chrysalis stage and emerge as an adult.

to distribute seeds nationwide, and more than 1 million seed packets have been given out since Save Our Monarchs launched in 2014.

The foundation seeks volunteer conservationists in cities across America. "We need more evangelists along the flyway," Ward says. "These people plant and influence others to plant milkweed. There are 114 evangelists across the country, but we'd love to add to that number!"

Monarch Joint Venture

In 2008, a number of ambassadors joined forces to create a powerhouse group that now has more than 45 passionate partners, including Monarch Watch, Journey North and Naturedigger as well as federal and state agencies and academic and nonprofit programs.

"These partners work together to effectively restore habitat for butterflies and pollinators across the country, to conduct high-priority research to better inform our conservation efforts, and to increase awareness through education and outreach," says Wendy Caldwell, Monarch Joint Venture coordinator.

The goal of Monarch Joint Venture is to provide an information clearinghouse so everyone involved in conservation stays up to date. Many of the venture's partners participate in similar efforts, such as researching and monitoring behavior; conserving, restoring and enhancing habitat; and educating and reaching out through workshops, websites, social media, videos and other means. As people work together, information is more readily available and

Grow swamp milkweed in Zones 3 to 8.

Not all milkweeds are created equal. Do a little research to find out which native species grow best in your area.

MAKE A DIFFERENCE
Here are a few easy ways you can lend a helping hand.

• **Plant milkweed.** "We need an estimated 1 billion to 1.5 billion additional milkweed stems on the landscape to reach our nation's target population size by 2020," advocate Wendy Caldwell says. Most people think of common milkweed, but there are 76 native species of milkweed from which to choose.

• **Add nectar plants.** Adult butterflies need late-season nectar plants to fuel their migration. Ideally, these plants bloom all season long and are protected from wind.

• **Go natural.** "A healthy wildlife garden welcomes bugs, dragonflies, bats, toads, praying mantises and other creatures," says naturalist David Mizejewski. "The diversity of plants and animals keeps everything in check." Pesticides kill good bugs, too.

• **Be a citizen scientist.** "We have learned a lot about monarchs through contributions from citizen science volunteers," Wendy says. "Report your observations to existing programs and share this with anyone you can inspire to get involved."

• **Donate.** Financial support for conservation initiatives is important. "Every donation makes a difference and helps more butterflies take flight," Wendy says.

efforts to help monarchs increase tremendously. You can learn more about the project by visiting *monarchjointventure.org.*

National Wildlife Federation

No stranger to the monarch's plight, the National Wildlife Federation (NWF) shows a dedication to gardening for wildlife that is vital when it comes to these butterflies. As a partner of the Monarch Joint Venture and the U.S. Fish and Wildlife Service, NWF works to increase populations and ensure that these beauties are here to stay.

"Conventional gardening advice has said to eliminate milkweed," says David Mizejewski, a naturalist with NWF. "It's a PR problem. Urban to suburban landscapers and big agriculture operations are removing milkweed and other nectar plants from landscapes, using harmful pesticides, especially along the central flyway."

The NWF is creating a monarch highway along the Interstate 35 corridor, running from Texas north through the Midwest, by restoring both habitat and milkweed along this crucial part of the butterfly's migratory map.

Another initiative is the Mayors' Monarch Pledge. Mayors or municipal leaders promise to plant more milkweed, use green space for pollinators and apply fewer insecticides. So far, more than 140 mayors have pledged.

The NWF's Butterfly Heroes program has enrolled thousands of people. Kids pledge to plant a garden with native plants and milkweed at their schools, parks and homes. In return, they receive a butterfly garden starter kit. Head to *nwf.org* for more information.

Master Milkweed in 5 Simple Steps

Help monarchs thrive by growing their favorite food in your yard. **By Jill Staake**

Where there are milkweeds, there are monarchs. Watch caterpillars chow down on the leaves and, later, follow mature butterflies as they fly from flower to flower sipping nectar. Use these tips to attract more monarchs with native milkweed.

1. Choose the right type for your garden.

The milkweed genus (*Asclepias*) has more than 140 species, and while all are native to the Americas, not all are the right fit for your garden. For instance, common milkweed (*Asclepias syriaca*) has a wide native range, but it can spread aggressively and may not be suited to a small yard. Call your county extension office to find out which milkweeds are native to your region, and take time to learn about their growth habits and requirements before deciding which to plant.

2. Seek out local plants or seeds.

Head to your area's native-plant nursery or find one near you at *plantnative.org*, then find out which milkweed plants it offers. To save money, ask friends for cuttings from their plants.

3. Sow seeds in fall, set out plants in spring.

If you're starting from seed, fall is the best time to broad-sow outdoors. Many varieties contain hard coatings that have to break down before the seeds germinate, and exposure to a winter's worth of snow and rain will do just that. If you're buying plants, add them to your garden in spring after the danger of frost has passed.

4. Trim early seedpods, save seeds from later ones.

Once a plant starts making seeds, it stops putting energy into producing leaves and flowers. Extend the growth time of your milkweed by trimming spent flowers through midsummer. Later in the season, collect seeds by tying small bags over the pods while they mature, since many burst open to distribute their seeds far and wide. Check out Monarch Watch at *monarchwatch.org* for more information on how to collect and care for milkweed seeds.

5. Learn to recognize caterpillars, eggs and possible pests.

Identify monarch caterpillars by their white, black and yellow stripes. The pinhead-size eggs are white and are laid singly on the tops or bottoms of leaves. Common pests include milkweed aphids. Tiny yellow specks with black legs, they are found by the dozens clustered near the plant stem. Remove aphids by hand or blast them with a garden hose if they're causing damage.

Monarch caterpillar

5 NATIVES TO TRY

- Common (*A. syriaca*)
- Butterfly weed (*A. tuberosa*)
- Swamp (*A. incarnata*)
- Showy (*A. speciosa*)
- Aquatic (*A. perennis*)

Swamp milkweed

FOLLOW THAT

Butterfly!

THESE 14 DESTINATIONS WILL LEAVE YOU FLOATING ON CLOUD NINE.
By Heather Lamb

THE BINOCULARS ARE PACKED UP and the map is laid out, but be sure to toss a butterfly field guide into your suitcase, too. There are more opportunities than ever for anyone with a bad case of wanderlust to go nose to antennae with exciting species. Most of the hot spots on this list favor native butterflies in seasonal settings, but there are some don't-miss stops for tropical species here, too. Whether you want to stand in the middle of a butterfly house teeming with a rainbow of activity, or take it easy in the great outdoors and watch these favorites of the insect world flutter on by, there's a destination for you.

Paper kite butterfly on Mexican flame vine

1

Purdy Butterfly House

HUNTSVILLE, ALABAMA

Stroll along any of the abundant walking paths in this 9,000-square-foot glass-enclosed butterfly house at the Huntsville Botanical Garden and see thousands of pollinators floating through the air. But don't forget to look down from time to time; frogs and turtles frolic in ponds bordered by lush plantings. Open May through September.
hsvbg.org

2

Butterfly Pavilion

LOS ANGELES, CALIFORNIA

Get ready to be awed when you step inside the pavilion at the Natural History Museum of Los Angeles County, which showcases native California butterflies. Keep your eyes peeled for the state butterfly, the California dogface. A monarch way station is just outside the entrance, which means milkweed grows here to feed the caterpillars and to provide nectar for the migrating adult monarchs. Open in summer.
nhm.org

3

Natural Bridges State Beach

SANTA CRUZ, CALIFORNIA

Beautiful flowering eucalyptus trees transform this preserve into a gorgeous monarch grove from late fall through winter as 100,000 migrators seek shelter among the branches. Guides are available to help visitors understand the majesty of the monarchs' flight. The ethereal insects typically overwinter mid-October through late January.
www.parks.ca.gov

Hot spots on this list host species such as monarch and white peacock butterflies.

Watch for tropical species at Butterfly World in Coconut Creek, Florida.

Blue morpho butterfly

The Day Butterfly Center is in a glass conservatory.

4
Butterfly World
COCONUT CREEK, FLORIDA

This butterfly house opened in 1988, making it one of the oldest in the U. S. It features an impressive array of tropical and native species. Birders get the bonus of two aviaries on-site, too. Open year-round. *butterflyworld.com*

5
Arnold's Butterfly Haven
LAKE OKEECHOBEE, FLORIDA

Although this open-air exhibit is small, at only a half-acre, it's big on ingenuity. Planted in the shape of a zebra longwing, Florida's state butterfly, the garden uses extensive host and nectar plants to attract free-flying species. In fact, more than 50 have been spotted here. Open year-round. *arnoldsbutterflyhaven.com*

6
Day Butterfly Center
PINE MOUNTAIN, GEORGIA

Catch the awe-inspiring sight of more than 1,000 tropical butterflies winging throughout this elegant glass conservatory at Callaway Gardens. The striking blue morphos that emerge in September make it a must-see. Open year-round. *callawaygardens.com*

7
Butterfly House at Botanica Gardens
WICHITA, KANSAS

Find garden inspiration among the nectar and host plants at this exhibit. The flowers act as colorful magnets for 50 native and tropical species in the 2,500-square-foot netted space. Open June through September. *botanica.org*

White morpho butterfly

Lena Meijer Tropical Conservatory

Small tortoiseshell butterfly

CLOCKWISE FROM TOP: FREDERIK MEIJER GARDENS & SCULPTURE PARK; WILLIAM J. HEBERT/FREDERIK MEIJER GARDENS & SCULPTURE

Hecale longwing

12

National Butterfly Center
MISSION, TEXAS

Located in the Lower Rio Grande Valley, the North American Butterfly Association's butterfly center is a park that features acres of plantings to attract local species. The city of Mission is home to the annual Texas Butterfly Festival in late October. Open year-round.
nationalbutterflycenter.org

13

Flying Flowers at Beagle Ridge Herb Farm
WYTHEVILLE, VIRGINIA

Native butterflies flutter around an enclosure, while an additional 2 acres at the herb farm host even more species. More than 30 types have been recorded in the outdoor gardens alone. Open spring through October.
beagleridgeherbfarm.com

14

Smithsonian Butterfly Habitat Garden
WASHINGTON, D.C.

Take a break from touring national monuments with a stop at this 11,000-square-foot garden. The space at the National Museum of Natural History emphasizes the relationships between butterflies and plants, with four distinct garden areas—wetland, meadow, urban garden and woodland edge. It's perfect for providing ideas for home gardeners. Open year-round.
gardens.si.edu

BUTTERFLY ETIQUETTE
Enclosed spaces and abundant fliers mean that lovely insects often land on visitors. To increase the chances for a thrilling close encounter, naturalist Wayne Richards has a few tips.

First, perfumes are a no-no. The same goes for smoke odor, because nicotine is poison to pollinators. Visit on a cloudy day if possible. Butterflies will often perch longer when the sun isn't shining. And those beads of perspiration that form in the houses' humid environment? It's a good thing. "Butterflies like sweaty people," Richards says. So embrace that sweatiness—the butterflies will thank you.

GARDENING FOR BIRDS, BUTTERFLIES & BEES

Plant picks for a wildlife-friendly backyard.

Attract Baltimore orioles with fruit-bearing shrubs like chokecherry, raspberry and serviceberry.

The importance of a garden goes far beyond its beauty. Purposefully choosing flowers, trees and shrubs to attract and sustain wildlife greatly benefits the environment and all the creatures in it. For over 20 years, *Birds & Blooms* has championed the idea of gardening with a purpose, and we put together a book about how to transform your backyard into a healthier, happier sanctuary for birds, butterflies and bees.

The next few pages offer a sampling of the book *Gardening for Birds, Butterflies & Bees*, complete with plant picks to guide you in your choices. Handy symbols indicate which creatures the plant attracts (birds, butterflies and/or bees) and whether the plant grows in full sun, part shade or shade.

Beyond suggesting plants, the book highlights more than 60 bird and 34 butterfly species you might see in your yard. Happy gardening!

PASSIONFLOWER
Passiflora spp., Zones 5 to 9

Not only does this quirky flower look cool, it's also a big draw for southern wildlife. Nectar-seekers visit blossoms, while certain types of longwings and other butterflies lay their eggs on the vine. The fragrant flowers come in shades of purple, blue, red, pink, yellow and white. The flowers make way for berries that birds devour. Vines range in length from 15 to 50 feet. Most gardeners let the tendrils climb walls and fences; others use it as ground cover.

AGASTACHE

Agastache spp., Zones 4 to 11

Bushy and studded with blooms from mid- to late summer, agastache is a favorite of hummingbirds, butterflies and bees. Flower spires in violet, orange, yellow, pink or blue reach 2 to 6 feet high. Agastache thrives in full sun and in well-draining, fertile soil.

CORAL BELLS

Heuchera sanguinea, Zones 3 to 8

Wands of red bell-shaped flowers and handsome, sometimes evergreen foliage make this bloomer a valuable addition to any garden, in sun or shade. Use this adaptable mounding plant along borders or in containers to attract more hummingbirds to your yard. Extend coral bells' blooming season by clipping off spent stems.

GLOBE THISTLE

Echinops ritro, Zones 3 to 9

Butterflies will be anything but blue when you plant this spiny azure beauty in your garden. Standing up to 2 feet tall, globe thistle, also known as blue hedgehog, grows best in poor but well-draining soil and full sun. Butterflies, bees and moths relish the nectar, and once seed heads form, finches and other birds will stop by to eat.

COREOPSIS

Coreopsis spp., Zones 3 to 11

Though you can find annual varieties of this graceful plant that are easy to grow from seed, make sure you pick up one of the perennial versions, too. Coreopsis loves the sun and grows well in dry conditions. A rainbow of new varieties, such as the bright pink shown here, offer striking alternatives to the traditional yellow blooms. Plants range from 8 to 48 inches high. Butterflies love the flowers, and songbirds eat the seeds.

BLAZING STAR

Liatris spp., Zones 3 to 9

The nectar of this spiky plant is a favorite of butterflies, especially the silver-spotted skipper. After the flowers fade, birds favor the seeds. The plants are easy to pick out in the garden—they reach up to 6 feet tall! Some types, like Kobold, are much shorter, measuring roughly 18 inches.

CLEMATIS

Clematis spp., Zones 4 to 9

By September, many clematis varieties are petering out, but other species, such as golden (*C. tangutica*) and sweet autumn clematis (*C. terniflora*), are at their peak. Either way, clematis is a fall wildlife winner, because once the petals fall, birds seek out the spindly seed clusters.

CONEFLOWER

Echinacea spp., Zones 3 to 9

Birds, bees and butterflies, including fritillaries, truly love this perennial! You'll see songbirds pause to nibble the seeds, and butterflies and hummers stopping for its nectar into the fall season. In winter, the remaining seed heads leave an interesting garden focal point.

SEDUM

Sedum spp., Zones 3 to 10

Many cultivars of this late-season favorite boast bold foliage, ranging from red to purple to gold. Other types of this versatile succulent, including the popular Autumn Joy, have broccoli-shaped, light green flower heads that slowly change to pink and deepen to burgundy; later, the seeds nourish songbirds. Most sedums are hardy in all but the harshest climates.

BEE BALM
Monarda spp., Zones 3 to 9

Also known as bergamot, this unusual beauty grows up to 4 feet tall and starts flowering in midsummer, inviting hummingbirds, butterflies and bees to your flower bed. Plants come in hues of pink, red, white and purple; choose mildew-resistant varieties for best results. Frequent deadheading will keep this enthusiastic self-sower in check, but then you won't see songbirds stopping to eat the seeds once petals die back. The choice is yours!

LAVENDER
Lavandula spp., Zones 5 to 10

In the summertime, hummingbirds, skippers, painted ladies and other pollinators frequently visit lavender. You'll love this Mediterranean bloomer for its attractive flower spires, silvery-green foliage and calming scent. Varieties of this flower grow from 1 to 4 feet tall, and are available in many shades of purple, as well as in white and light pink.

HOLLYHOCK
Alcea rosea, Zones 3 to 9

If you want to make an impact in your garden, look no further than this plant, which is a host to butterfly larvae including hairstreaks, skippers and painted ladies. It comes in many colors, attracts a variety of insects and hummingbirds, and can reach 8 feet. Hollyhock is a biennial—growing foliage on short stems its first year, flowering the next year. Then it seeds itself.

ORIENTAL POPPY
Papaver orientale, Zones 2 to 9

This plant can be difficult to grow—it doesn't handle transplanting well and it requires a sunny site with adequately draining soil. But the Oriental poppy's vibrant, papery blooms are worth the effort. In the right location, this exotic-looking flower fills in quickly and rewards gardeners with years of enjoyment.

a buzzworthy

Plants like lungwort help honeybees and various native bee species to thrive.

CAUSE

Help the declining pollinator population and become a bee champion. **By Crystal Rennicke**

BEES ARE A BIG DEAL. These unsung heroes of the planet work hard to keep our food web functioning. One in every three bites of food we eat is courtesy of pollination, and 85 percent of flowering plants and trees rely on pollinators for survival.

A Sticky Situation

Many people are concerned about the decline of honeybee populations. Since 2006, Colony Collapse Disorder has wiped out nearly 3 million hives. According to the Centre for Research on Globalization in Montreal, Canada, the honeybee population has dropped by more than 30 percent. In addition, many of the 4,000 species of native bees are in decline, some verging on extinction. What happened?

A bee hotel provides shelter for bees to raise their young.

"All bee species face similar stressors—poor nutrition due to a lack of flowers or monocropping, pesticide exposure, parasites and diseases," says Phyllis Stiles, director of Bee City USA, a certification program that helps pollinator populations. "It's important to understand that pollinator-plant relationship because it directly affects our food."

Hope for a Better Future

What can gardeners do to help our bees? "Plant native plants, trees and shrubs, reduce lawns and expand the natural areas in your yard," Phyllis says.

Cultivate a PC (pollinator-conscious) backyard by eliminating pesticides or using safer ones, such as *Bacillus thuringiensis* (*Bt*). Choose plants from local nurseries that don't treat seeds with neonicotinoid pesticides, which kill all insects by attacking the central nervous system.

Another beneficial action is to create nesting and overwintering spots for pollinators. "Seventy percent of bee species nest in the ground," Phyllis says. "Reserving areas of dry, bare, undisturbed ground provides places for them to raise their young in the early spring."

The remaining 30 percent of native bees nest in tunnels in stumps and snags, so leave some stumps and dead wood in your landscape. Drill holes in blocks of untreated lumber for bee habitats. If you're feeling especially hospitable, erect a bee hotel, a structure with stacked, narrow tubes that mimics a bee's natural living quarters. Avoid placing the bee hotel in shade, which might attract unwanted wasps. Have it facing southeast. Bees like to be warm in the morning before heading out to gather pollen.

And become an advocate: Petition for a community or school garden, and campaign to have native plants in public spaces.

Butterfly weed does double duty: Both bees and butterflies love it.

eekeeper—buy local honey!

Bees visit Ozark coneflowers for pollen and nectar.

BECOME A BEE CITY

Thanks to organizations such as Bee City USA, the future looks sweeter for our pollinators. Launched in 2012, the Bee City USA program supports the creation of sustainable habitats for pollinators.

"Each city needs at least one champion to build a coalition for applying for Bee City USA certification," says Phyllis. "This champion can be a city staff person, a beekeeper, a city council member, the mayor or a gardener. He or she simply has to present the case for certification to fellow citizens."

Certification from Bee City USA is both an honor and a responsibility. After certification, each Bee City has an annual celebration, usually coinciding with National Pollinator Week in June, that includes educational activities.

Currently there are 15 Bee City communities in the U.S. Find out more at *beecityusa.org*.

10 Plants for Pollinators

Try some or all of these to welcome bees to your yard. For plants specific to your growing region, check the USDA database at *plants.usda.gov* or ask at your local nursery.

1 Phlox
Phlox paniculata, Zones 3 to 9
This hardy native perennial has fragrant, blue-pink blooms in mid- to late summer.

2 Cardinal flower
Lobelia, Zones 3 to 9
A native perennial that grows up to 3 feet, this plant has showy red blooms in mid- to late summer and into fall.

3 Aster
Aster, Zones 4 to 9
The aster is a late fall plant that's important for pre-hibernation bumblebee queens. Blue, lavender, pink or white flowers look lovely as ground cover, along borders or in containers.

4 Coneflower
Echinacea purpurea,
Zones 3 to 8
This native wildflower is simple to grow and has masses of tall purple blooms. Recent cultivars come in other colors, but stick with natives for the most nectar value.

5 Joe Pye weed
Eupatorium purpureum,
Zones 3 to 9
Primarily known as a butterfly plant, this perennial also attracts bees with its fragrant pink-purple blooms. It prefers moist soil, where it can shoot up to 9 feet tall.

6 Blazing star
Liatris, Zones 3 to 9
These purple or white beauties support a broad community of butterflies, including monarchs, swallowtails, skippers and sulphurs. They grow up to 3 feet tall.

7 Sunflower
Helianthus, annual
Sunflowers are a favorite of many bee species. Easy to establish and tolerant of most soils, sunflowers can grow almost anywhere.

8 Goldenrod
Solidago, Zones 3 to 10
With its feathery yellow blossoms, goldenrod provides late-season forage for honeybees, bumblebees, butterflies, beneficial wasps, soldier beetles and more.

9 Black-eyed Susan
Rudbeckia, Zones 3 to 10
Its bright yellow blooms and dark brown centers offer a cheery spot for bees and other insects. Some varieties feature orange and red petals or bicolored blooms.

10 Bee balm
Monarda, Zones 3 to 10
Bee balm is a vigorous native that boasts fragrant purple, pink, red or white flowers. Despite its name, it also attracts butterflies and hummingbirds.

DID YOU KNOW? Alkali bees (shown here) look similar to honeybees, but they're slightly smaller.

The Good Bees

Help these beneficial insects thrive in your backyard. **By David Mizejewski**

Bees are tremendously important pollinators of plants, commercial crops and native vegetation. There are over 4,000 native North American bee species, in addition to the European honeybee, and many are in decline. Most native bees are solitary, individually nesting in tunnels rather than forming hives and making honey.

To create a bee-friendly space, plant wildflowers, blooming trees and shrubs for a steady supply of nectar and pollen from early spring to fall. Fill a birdbath with gravel to give bees a place to drink without drowning, and another filled with mud for nesting material. Provide fallen logs, tree snags, dead plant stems and open patches of sandy soil for nesting. Plus, you can build or buy bee houses made of replaceable nesting tubes. Once you've got these few basics down and bees are visiting your yard, watch for some of these species:

Squash Bees

These fuzzy, solitary ground nesters gather nectar and pollen exclusively from squash, pumpkins and gourds, pollinating the flowers so the plants can produce bounty for you.

Mason Bees

There are about 140 mason bee species in North America. Some have dull black and yellow striping, while others are blue-black or green. They are solitary nesters, laying eggs in a series of mud-walled chambers in decaying wood. The blue orchard mason bee is an efficient pollinator of fruit trees.

Blueberry Bees

Blueberry bees are a stocky, solitary species and look similar to bumblebees. They vibrate their wings at a blossom to shake the pollen out of it, a technique called "buzz pollination." They are important pollinators of blueberries in the South.

Alkali Bees

Crucial to the pollination of alfalfa, these boldly striped bees are found

Bee houses provide shelter and a safe place to nest for many species, like this mason bee.

Squash bee

14 plants for bees
Create an ideal bee habitat with nectar and pollen plants.

- Milkweed
- Mountain mint
- Anise hyssop
- Sedum
- Lavender
- Blanket flower
- Bee balm
- Coneflower

- Sunflower
- Aster
- Blueberry
- Elderberry
- Serviceberry
- Apple, pear and other fruit trees

Golden northern bumblebee

in the West and nest in tunnels in the ground. Though they don't form hives, females build their elaborate nesting tunnels in close proximity to each other, forming colonies.

Bumblebees
Like honeybees, bumblebees form hives. There are 46 species in North America, and most nest in holes in the ground, under fallen logs or in old rodent burrows. In the spring, the queen emerges from hibernation and looks for a suitable place to build her hive. She mated at the end of the previous summer and is ready to lay her first eggs, which hatch into female worker bees that collect nectar and pollen, make honey and maintain the hive. Bumblebees pollinate native wildflowers and several edibles, such as tomatoes, peppers and strawberries.

Southeastern blueberry bee

Meet the Mantids

Get up close and personal with these mysterious backyard hunters.
By David Mizejewski

Maybe you've spotted a mantis clinging to a thin branch or skulking in a thick garden hedge. With front legs folded in what looks like prayer, these large-bodied insects are fun to look at—and hard to miss. Throw in their unusual behavior, like cocking their heads sideways and hunting prey big and small, and praying mantises become some of the fiercest and most fascinating bugs in your garden.

Well over a thousand mantid species crawl across the globe, but only a handful live in North America. Collectively, they go by the catchall term "praying mantis" because of the way the insect holds its forelimbs in front of its thorax. But that serene posture can be deceiving: While it may seem to be in deep meditation, it's actually waiting for an unsuspecting insect to venture too close.

Mantids typically eat other bugs but aren't too picky about dinner. If a fellow garden visitor passes near enough, they instinctively try to grab it and make a meal of it. While this

does mean that praying mantises will consume beneficial insects, like butterflies and bees, they're also happy to dine on pests like mosquitoes and flies. In the grand scheme, mantises feast on more bad bugs than good bugs, and it's much more natural to rely on them to do the dirty work of controlling pesky insect populations than it is to spray toxic pesticides.

The praying mantis life cycle takes about a year. Females reach full size by mid- to late summer, when they are

CLOCKWISE FROM LEFT: CULTURA CREATIVE (RF)/ALAMY STOCK PHOTO; GERALD HOLMES, CALIFORNIA POLYTECHNIC STATE UNIVERSITY AT SAN LUIS OBISPO, BUGWOOD.ORG;

More on Mantids

Although the praying mantis is a welcome backyard guest, one species in particular overstays its welcome: Chinese mantids. They're eye-catching, but these invasive insects are replacing native species such as the Carolina mantid. The situation is not complete gloom and doom, though. Like all mantids, this species eats pesky garden bugs, too.

Chinese mantid

DID YOU KNOW?
Mantids inspired several styles of Chinese martial arts, including northern praying mantis kung fu.

ready to mate. The males, which are a lot smaller, proceed with caution, because cannibalism isn't unknown in mantid species. After mating, the female lays a cluster of eggs on a plant stem and encases them in foam that dries into a protective case. The eggs overwinter and develop. Then, come springtime, they hatch into miniature replicas of the adults, ready to devour any garden pests that come their way.

No matter where you live, the best way to persuade mantids to settle in your garden or landscape is simply to fill your space with a wide range of plants. Native plants work best because they more readily attract tasty insects. Avoid insecticides, too, and you are well on your way to a praying mantis paradise.

Giant swallowtail
Finalist in our
Backyard Photo Contest
Photo by Roslynn Long

Spicebush swallowtail
Finalist in our
Backyard Photo Contest
Photo by Amy Bosse

Monarch butterfly
*Photo by Bill McMullen/
Getty Images*

Eastern tiger swallowtail
Finalist in our
Backyard Photo Contest
Photo by Linda Van Zandvoord

Gulf fritillary
Finalist in our
Backyard Photo Contest
Photo by Deb Henson

Native Plants Chart

Attract more birds and butterflies by including native plants in your landscape.

	COMMON NAME	SCIENTIFIC NAME	HARDINESS ZONES	FLOWER COLOR	HEIGHT	BLOOM TIME	SOIL MOISTURE
DRY SOILS AND DRY CLIMATES (15"–25" ANNUAL PRECIPITATION)	Leadplant	Amorpha canescens	3-8	Purple	2′ - 3′	June-July	D, M
	Butterfly weed	Asclepias tuberosa	3-10	Orange	2′ - 3′	June-Aug.	D, M
	Smooth aster	Aster laevis	4-8	Blue	2′ - 4′	Aug.-Oct.	D, M
	Cream false indigo	Baptisia bracteata	4-9	Cream	1′ - 2′	May-June	D, M
	Purple prairie clover	Dalea purpurea	3-8	Purple	1′ - 2′	July-Aug.	D, M
	Pale purple coneflower	Echinacea pallida	4-8	Purple	3′ - 5′	June-July	D, M
	Prairie smoke	Geum triflorum	3-6	Pink	6″	May-June	D, M
	Dotted blazing star	Liatris punctata	3-9	Purple/Pink	1′ - 2′	Aug.-Oct.	D, M
	Wild lupine	Lupinus perennis	3-8	Blue	1′ - 2′	May-June	D
	Large-flowered beardtongue	Penstemon grandiflorus	3-7	Lavender	2′ - 4′	May-June	D
	Showy goldenrod	Solidago speciosa	3-8	Yellow	1′ - 3′	Aug.-Sept.	D, M
	Bird's-foot violet	Viola pedata	3-9	Blue	6″	Apr.-June	D
MEDIUM SOILS IN AVERAGE RAINFALL CLIMATES (25"–45" ANNUAL PRECIPITATION)	Nodding pink onion	Allium cernuum	3-8	White/Pink	1′ - 2′	July-Aug.	M, Mo
	New England aster	Aster novae-angliae	3-7	Blue/Purple	3′ - 6′	Aug.-Sept.	M, Mo
	Blue false indigo	Baptisia australis	3-10	Blue	3′ - 5′	June-July	M, Mo
	White false indigo	Baptisia lactea	4-9	White	3′ - 5′	June-July	M, Mo
	Shooting star	Dodecatheon meadia	4-8	White/Pink	1′ - 2′	May-June	M, Mo
	Purple coneflower	Echinacea purpurea	4-8	Purple	3′ - 4′	July-Sept.	M, Mo
	Rattlesnake master	Eryngium yuccifolium	4-9	White	3′ - 5′	June-Aug.	M
	Prairie blazing star	Liatris pycnostachya	3-9	Purple/Pink	3′ - 5′	July-Aug.	M, Mo
	Wild quinine	Parthenium integrifolium	4-8	White	3′ - 5′	June-Sept.	M, Mo
	Yellow coneflower	Ratibida pinnata	3-9	Yellow	3′ - 6′	July-Sept.	M, Mo
	Royal catchfly	Silene regia	4-9	Red	2′ - 4′	July-Aug.	M
	Stiff goldenrod	Solidago rigida	3-9	Yellow	3′ - 5′	Aug.-Sept.	M, Mo
MOIST SOILS AND MOIST CLIMATES (45"–60" ANNUAL PRECIPITATION)	Wild hyacinth	Camassia scilloides	4-8	White	1′ - 2′	May-June	M, Mo
	Tall Joe Pye weed	Eupatorium fistulosum	4-9	Purple/Pink	5′ - 8′	Aug.-Sept.	Mo, W
	Queen of the prairie	Filipendula rubra	3-6	Pink	4′ - 5′	June-July	M, Mo
	Bottle gentian	Gentiana andrewsii	3-6	Blue	1′ - 2′	Aug.-Oct.	Mo, W
	Rose mallow	Hibiscus palustris	4-9	Pink	3′ - 6′	July-Sept.	Mo, W
	Dense blazing star	Liatris spicata	4-10	Purple/Pink	3′ - 6′	Aug.-Sept.	Mo, W
	Cardinal flower	Lobelia cardinalis	3-9	Red	2′ - 5′	July-Sept.	Mo, W
	Marsh phlox	Phlox glaberrima	4-8	Red/ Purple	2′ - 4′	June-July	M, Mo
	Sweet black-eyed Susan	Rudbeckia subtomentosa	3-9	Yellow	4′ - 6′	Aug.-Oct.	M, Mo
	Ohio goldenrod	Solidago ohioensis	4-5	Yellow	3′ - 4′	Aug.-Sept.	M, Mo
	Tall ironweed	Vernonia altissima	4-9	Red/Pink	5′ - 8′	Aug.-Sept.	Mo, W
	Culver's root	Veronicastrum virginicum	3-8	White	3′ - 6′	July-Aug.	M, Mo

SOIL MOISTURE KEY

D = Dry (Well-draining sandy and rocky soils), **M** = Medium (Normal garden soils such as loam, sandy loam and clay loam),
Mo = Moist (Soils that stay moist below the surface, but are not boggy; may dry out in late summer),
W = Wet (Soils that are continually moist through the growing season, subject to short periods of spring flooding)

What's Your Zone?
Plant Hardiness Zone Map

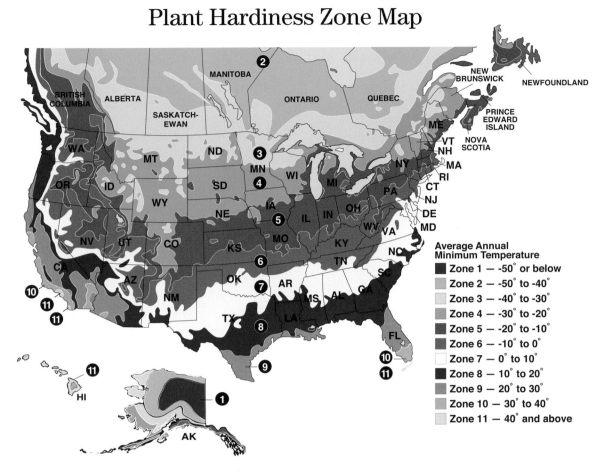

Average Annual Minimum Temperature

Zone 1 — -50° or below
Zone 2 — -50° to -40°
Zone 3 — -40° to -30°
Zone 4 — -30° to -20°
Zone 5 — -20° to -10°
Zone 6 — -10° to 0°
Zone 7 — 0° to 10°
Zone 8 — 10° to 20°
Zone 9 — 20° to 30°
Zone 10 — 30° to 40°
Zone 11 — 40° and above

Plant Heat Zone Map

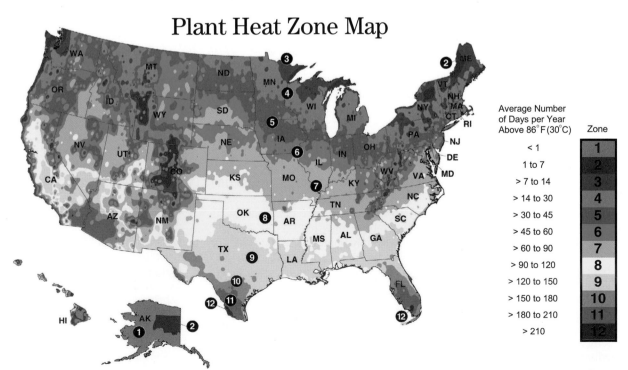

Average Number of Days per Year Above 86° F (30°C) — Zone

Days	Zone
< 1	1
1 to 7	2
> 7 to 14	3
> 14 to 30	4
> 30 to 45	5
> 45 to 60	6
> 60 to 90	7
> 90 to 120	8
> 120 to 150	9
> 150 to 180	10
> 180 to 210	11
> 210	12

Index

"Once it has a toehold,
incongruity has a
way of advancing
systematically
through the garden
like quackgrass."

—Des Kennedy
Crazy About Gardening